Famous Men of
Greece

by John H. Haaren, LL.D.
& A.B. Poland, Ph.D.

Revised, Edited, and Updated by
Cyndy A. Shearer & Robert G. Shearer

Greenleaf Press
Lebanon, Tennessee

Published by

Greenleaf Books, LLC

Tenth Printing, February, 2000

3761 Highway 109 N., Unit D,
Lebanon, TN 37087
Phone: 615-449-1617

History for the thoughtful child

Table of Contents

Famous Men of Greece
Preface

When our eldest child was four we decided to school him at home. We spent the next year haunting curriculum fairs, and book sales. We made nuisances of ourselves at the homes of other homeschoolers wanting to look at their books. We found good reading texts, reasonable math texts, even science texts we liked (once we learned skip everything written for K-second). But we could not find a history text or program that satisfied us (maybe it's because one of us had spent ten years studying and teaching European history).

We looked everywhere for a curriculum/text that would begin at the beginning and present history in a logical, readable, chronological way. We tried hard, but we never found one. **The Famous Men** series was our solution to our own need.

Existing history texts for the early years are, for the most part, filled with what Charlotte Mason called "twaddle." The most pressing bit of information conveyed in the majority of social studies texts is "you live in America" and "the fireman (policeman, doctor, librarian) is your friend." These things, we believe, any non-comatose child knows long before kindergarten. Current textbooks are little more than world sociology with training wheels. They have no history, and no geography, just a sociological tour of countries: Pablo of Brazil, Yuki, boy of Tokyo. Some "real" American history might begin in the fifth grade, with world history covered in the sixth. But then most textbooks repeat American history all over again in the seventh, eighth and ninth grades.

Think about that sequence for a minute...

It seemed to us very odd to spend three years studying 200 years and one year cramming down the other couple of thousand (If it's November we must be in Medieval Europe). We longed for a program that would begin at the beginning. When our children began to study American history we wanted them to know where the country came from.

V.M. Hilyer, late headmaster of the Calvert School, had a similar desire when he wrote <u>A Child's History of the World</u> (currently out of print). In his introduction to that book he writes:

> "In common with all children of my age, I was brought up on American
> History and given no other history but American, year in and year out,
> year after year for eight or more years.
> So far as I knew 1492 was the beginning of the world. Any events or char-
> acters before that time, reference to which I encountered by any chance,
> were put down in my mind in the same category with fairy tales. Christ
> and His times, of which I heard only in Sunday school, were to me mere fic-
> tion without reality. They were not mentioned in any history that I knew
> and therefore, so I thought, must belong <u>not</u> to a realm in time and space,
> but to a spiritual realm."

In organizing a course of study for our children, we chose to break with the tradition that attempts to condense the study of world history into a one year course. We decided to spread the material out over the elementary school years and proceed at a leisurely pace that would allow the child to "live with" the material for a period of months. By the time the child has completed the seventh grade he should have covered the full span of world and American history and thus be ready to begin again in greater depth a study of History and the Humanities at the high school level.

It is not our expectation that the seventh grader will necessarily remember every minute detail and date he learned about Egypt in his second grade year. But rather, that when he comes across references to events and people in his later studies, he finds himself in familiar territory with background knowledge he can draw from or build upon.

There are two important strands in the teaching of history, necessary to making it an enjoyable, living study. First, children learn best by doing (making of models, retelling stories, recitation, play-making). For this reason, we begin the study of every new area by making a salt relief map. The child must study a map and note geographical features that his map will need to include. Then he must draw it and shape the dough into the drawing — making mountains and rivers and valleys. Once this is done, geography is no longer an abstraction, but something he has had his own hands in.

The second principle behind our approach is that children are fascinated by real people who have real adventures. When we read about Moses leading a rebellious and grumbling people across a desert, we identify with Moses. When we read the story to our children, our children identify with Moses — until it is not only Moses that we see, but ourselves, acting under seemingly impossible circumstances. The study of history becomes not merely the study of nations, but a moral training ground where the wise and the unwise are observed, and the consequences of wisdom and folly may be dissected under a teacher who charges less than experience.

Just as the child identifies with Moses, he can also identify with other historical figures and analyze the wisdom and folly of their actions. When at the center of all this is the question, **"What does God think about this action, person, behavior?"**, then the study of history (even the study of very pagan nations) takes place in a way in which the God of History is ever present.

When God wanted to teach His people their history, He taught them about the lives of specific individuals. There are lessons to be learned from the good kings (virtue to imitate) and the rotten kings (sins to avoid). The Bible is also brutally realistic in recording the failings of the good guys and the occasional (if only accidental) virtues of the wicked. The history of the Old Testament is not a long dry procession of dates to memorize and unfamiliar names to fill in blanks, but the life stories of people who interest us.

We are firmly convinced that biography should be an integral part of a child's study of history. That is why we have published Famous Men of Greece, Famous Men of Rome, Famous Men of the Middle Ages, and Famous Men of the Renaissance & Reformation. We hope your children will enjoy these stories as much as ours have.

There is a companion Study Guide also available from Greenleaf Press which is intended to be used in conjunction with this book. **The Study Guide** includes vocabulary, pronunciation guides, and discussion questions for each chapter and suggests a number of supplemental readings from other books. **The Study Guide** may be ordered directly from Greenleaf Press.

In addition to Greenleaf Press publications, we also carry a variety of good history books for children from other publishers. Our catalog includes other books, tapes, and videos that will help you build your own history curriculum, unit study, or Konos theme study. The history titles are grouped by major historical period, so you can see all the titles for the periods you are interested in easily.

Cynthia A. Shearer & Robert G. Shearer

For a free copy of the Greenleaf Press Catalog, write to us at:
Greenleaf Press
3761 Highway 109 N., Unit D,
Lebanon, TN 37087
or call us at:
Phone: **615-449-1617**
Fax: **615-449-4018**
Email: **Greenleafp@aol.com**

or visit our Website at: **http://www.greenleafpress.com**

Original Preface
1904 Edition

The study of history, like the study of a landscape, should begin with the most conspicuous features. Not until these have been fixed in memory will the lesser features fall into their appropriate places and assume their right proportions.

In order to attract and hold the child's attention, each conspicuous feature of history presented to him should have an individual for its center. The child identifies himself with the person placed before him. It is not Romulus or Hercules or Caesar or Alexander that the child has in mind when he reads, but himself, acting under the prescribed conditions.

Prominent educators, appreciating these truths, have long recognized the value of biography as a preparation for the study of history and have given it an important place in their schools.

The former practice in many elementary schools of beginning the detailed study of American history without any previous knowledge of general history limited the pupil's range of vision, restricted his sympathies, and left him without material for comparisons. Moreover, it denied to him a knowledge of his inheritance from the Greek philosopher, the Roman lawgiver, the Teutonic lover of freedom. Hence our recommendation that the study of Greek, Roman and modern European history in the form of biography should precede the study of detailed American history in our elementary schools.

It has been the aim of the author to make an interesting story of each man's life and to tell these stories in a style so simple that pupils in the lower grades will read them with pleasure, and so dignified that they may be used with profit as textbooks for reading.

Introduction

THE GODS OF GREECE

Part I

If you were to have asked a citizen of ancient Greece to tell you something about the history of his nation, he would have wanted to begin at what he would have considered to be the beginning. He would have begun by telling you about his gods and the myths and legends told about them. Even though the events described in the myths did not actually happen in the way the story says, myths will tell you much about what was important to the people who told them.

As the ancient Greek citizen told of things that occurred closer to his own time, the stories would begin to include things that might possibly have happened. Stories that are told about people that may have lived, or events that may have happened, such as the stories about the Trojan war, are called legends. In a legend the facts about a person or an event are mixed up with make-believe. There may have been a person named Hercules, or Theseus who was a very brave and respected leader. But as more people tell stories about a legendary hero, the things that were true are exaggerated, and new adventures and abilities are added, until it becomes harder to separate the real facts from the make believe.

As the citizen of ancient Greece came even closer in time to his own day, the stories he would tell you would be stories about people who really did live and events that really did happen. As you read this book, you will find examples of myths, legends, and facts. You will want to learn to recognize the differences between each type of story. As you read, ask yourself, "What things in this story could have really happened?"

The people of ancient Greece considered themselves to be very religious. They worshipped many gods. The gods that they worshipped acted very much like extra big and extra strong human beings. The gods were often selfish and jealous. They argued and fought. If they got angry enough, they could throw very big temper tantrums. Often men and women found themselves caught in the middle of those tantrums. Though the gods possessed great power, they were not invincible and could be outsmarted by clever men. Nonetheless, the Greek people took their worship very seriously. That's the reason the citizen of Greece would want to introduce you to his gods and tell you something about their stories. The first stories he would have told you would have been about the Titans.

Exactly when the Titans came to be, no one could say. Their size and strength was tremendous all the same. It is from the name, Titan, that we get the word titanic, meaning something that is unusually large. One Titan was named Hy-per´i-on. He was said to be the father of the sun, moon and dawn. Another Titan, Ipetus, had two sons — Atlas, who bore the weight of the earth on his shoulders, and Prometheus, who angered the gods of Olympus by giving men the gift of fire. But the greatest of the Titans, the one who ruled all others, was named Cro´nus.

Cronus had three sons, Zeus, Poseidon, and Hades. The three brothers overthrew their father and cast lots to see how they would divide the world. Zeus became king of the gods and men. He was also the god of the sky. In pictures of Zeus you will often see him holding great thunderbolts in his hand.

Top: *Poseidon rises from the sea to help the Greeks*
Bottom: *Poseidon and his horses*

Poseidon became the god of the seas. He held a three pointed spear, called a trident. With this trident he could shatter huge rocks, stir up great storms or calm them. It was said that Poseidon created horses and used them to draw his chariot across the top of the water. His horses had beautiful golden manes and hoofs of bronze. Whenever their brazen hoofs trampled upon the waves, the sea became calm.

The underground world of Hades was a dreary region. It was the home of the dead. Round it flowed a black river called the "Styx," or "Hateful." The only way to cross this river was in a ferry boat rowed by a silent boatman named Cha´ron. At the gateway of the underworld was the terrible watchdog Ker´be-rus, or as we spell the name, Cer´be-rus. When the old Greeks buried a person, they put a coin in his mouth and a barley-cake sweetened with honey in his hand. The coin was to pay Charon for taking the spirit across the Styx. The cake was to be thrown to Cerberus so that, while he was eating it, the spirit might pass unnoticed into the spirit land.

No goddess was willing to be Hades's wife and live in his world of gloom. So he was very lonely. One day he visited the upper world in his chariot drawn by four handsome coal black steeds. He saw a beautiful maiden, named Per-seph´o-ne, whom we call Pros´er-pine, gathering flowers in a meadow. Hades at once bore her off to his kingdom of darkness and married her. Thus she became the queen of the lower world.

This made life much pleasanter for Hades, but it was very hard for Proserpine. She loved sunshine and flowers, and she grieved for them so much that at last Zeus took pity upon her and persuaded Hades to let her come back to the land of light for a part of every year. When she made her yearly visits the flowers that she loved so dearly bloomed for her, the grass grew green, and it was spring. When the time came that she must return to Hades, all the flowers drooped and died, the grass turned brown, and bleak winter followed.

Top: Hades and Cerberus
Bottom: Hades carrying off Proserpine

The sisters of Zeus had a great deal to do in their fair kingdoms. Every spring and summer De´me-ter caused the different kinds of fruits and grains and flowers to grow. As she could not do all this work alone, she had thousands of beautiful maidens, called nymphs, to help her. There was a wood nymph in every tree to make its leaves green and glossy and to color its blossoms. There was a water nymph in every spring that bubbled out of the hills, and one in every stream that flowed through the valleys. The nymphs of the springs and brooks watered the plants and crops of Demeter and made them grow.

The second sister, Hes´ti-a, was given charge of the home and hearthstone. She kept fires burning on the hearth and gave warmth to both the family and to any strangers who might come to see them. In every city and town of Greece, a fire sacred to Hestia was always kept burning.

Left: *Zeus and Hera*
Above: *Athena*

Part II

In his kingdom of the sky, Zeus dwelt in splendor, but he was not always happy. Although Her´a, his queen, was lovely in face and form, she was more beautiful than good-tempered. Sometimes she and Zeus had bitter quarrels.

One of the sons of Zeus was named Her´mes or Mer´cu-ry. He wore golden sandals and carried a wonderful wand. On the heels of the sandals were wings with which he could fly through the air like a bird. Because he could travel so swiftly, he became the messenger of the gods.

Another son of Zeus was He-phaes´tus, whom the Romans called Vulcan. He was the god of fire and the friend of workers in metals. He had a great forge under Mount Et´na, and there he made wonderful things of iron and brass. The round eyed Cyclops were his blacksmiths. One day Hephaestus was rude to his father. To punish him, his father hurled him from heaven. Hephaestus fell upon rocks and broke his leg. Ever after that he was lame.

A´res, the terrible god of war, whom the Romans called Mars, was another son of Zeus. He delighted in battle and bloodshed.

A-pol´lo and his twin sister, Ar´te-mis, or Di-an´a were also children of Zeus. They were both beautiful. Apollo's beauty was so great that when we wish to say that a man is handsome in face and form, we say, "He is an Apollo." Apollo and Artemis were great favorites with Zeus. He made Apollo the god of the sun, and Artemis the goddess of the moon. To each he gave a silver bow, from which they shot arrows of light.

The most wonderful daughter of Zeus was A-the´na, whom the Romans called Mi-ner´va. One day the king of the gods had a headache from which he could get no relief. He sent for Hephaestus. When the great blacksmith arrived at his father's palace, Zeus said to him, "Split open my head with your axe." As soon as Hephaestus had done this, a maiden goddess, clothed in armor, sprang from the head of Zeus. The maiden was Athena, goddess of wisdom.

The Gifts of Athena and Poseidon

Part III

Most beautiful of all the goddesses was Aph´ro-di-te (Roman name: Ve´nus), who sprang from the foam of the sea. She was the goddess of love. Several of the gods wished to marry her. Zeus decided the matter strangely by giving her to Hephaestus, the ugliest of all the gods.

Aphrodite had a son named E´ros (Roman name: Cu´pid), the god of love. He carried a bow and arrows, and if one of his arrows pierced the heart of a mortal, that mortal fell in love.

There was a fair goddess named I´ris, who caused the rainbow to brighten dark storm clouds, and often bore messages from heaven to men.

There were also many other gods and goddesses. Three sisters were known as The Graces. They made mortals gracious and lovable, friendly and pleasant in their ways.

There were three other sisters called The Furies. Their forms were draped in black, and their hair was

Hera, Eros and Aphrodite

twined with serpents. They punished wicked people and gave them no peace as long as they lived.

Higher than all gods and goddesses were three weird sisters, called The Fates. Not even Zeus could change the plans of The Fates. Whatever they said must come to pass always happened. Whatever they said should not happen never took place. When a child was born, one of the sisters began to spin the thread of its life. The second sister decided how long the thread should be. The third sister cut the thread when the moment came for the life to end.

After men came to Greece and dwelt there, the gods and goddesses withdrew to the far away peaks of O-lym´pus, the highest mountain in Greece, and made their home there.

Chapter I

DEUCALION AND THE FLOOD

Upon Olympus there was for every god a shining palace of brass, built by He-phaes´tus and the Cyclops. Every day the gods gathered in the great banqueting hall of Zeus to feast upon ambrosia (a special food that only the gods were to eat) and drink nectar from the goblets of gold.

At the banquets they were served by a lovely maiden named He´be, who was the goddess of youth. While they feasted, Apollo played on his lyre and the Muses sang. The Muses were the nine goddesses of poetry, arts, and sciences. Even in our own language, playing and singing are called music in memory of them.

Sometimes the gods came down from Olympus to visit the men in Greece and taught them what we call the useful arts. Athena, the goddess of wisdom, showed them how to harness horses and plow the ground. She showed the women how to spin and weave.

Demeter, the great earth-mother who made the fields fruitful, showed the farmers how to sow wheat and barley. Then, when the grain was ripe, she taught the farmers' wives how to make bread.

Hephaestus taught the Greeks how to make plows, spades and hoes and many other things of iron and brass.

When the gods came down now and then from Olympus, they found that the early Greeks were very wicked. The kindness of the gods made them no better; so at last Zeus decided to destroy them by a flood.

A certain half god, half man, named Pro-me´the-us, or Forethought, warned the Greeks of their danger. The only person that heeded his warning was his own son, Deu-ca´li-on. With Pyr´rha, his wife, Deucalion got into an ark as soon as the rain began.

It rained all over Greece for days and days. The rivers and brooks overflowed. The valleys were filled. The trees disappeared. All but the highest mountains were covered, but Deucalion's ark rode safely. At last the rain ceased. For nine days the ark drifted about on the face of the water. Then it grounded.

When the waters had gone down somewhat, Deucalion and Pyrrha found that they were on one of the mountains of Greece, called Par-nas´sus. They left their ark and walked down the mountain. Of all the Greeks, only these two were left; and among the quiet hills and valleys near or far, not a living creature was to be seen. The loneliness made them fearful. Scarcely knowing where they went, they came suddenly upon a deep cleft in the rocks. Out of the cleft dense volumes of steam and gas were pouring. Deucalion, who was braver than his wife, peered into the cleft; and while he did so, a wonderful voice came from the depths.

It said, "Cast behind you the bones of your mother!"

"An oracle!" cried Pyrrha.

"An oracle it is!" Deucalion cried.

Long ages before the flood, the gods sometimes used to speak with men and give them advice about things that were going to happen. What they said was called an "oracle," a word that means something told by the gods to men.

So now Deucalion and Pyrrha felt sure that one of the gods was telling them something.

But they wondered what the words, "Cast behind you the bones of your mother" could mean. After a while Deucalion said, "Pyrrha, the earth is our mother."

"Very true," said she.

"Then," cried Deucalion, "the bones of our mother must be the stones of the earth."

Both now saw plainly that the oracle meant that they should cast behind them the stones that lay scattered upon the ground. So they went on down the mountain, and as they went they picked up stones which they cast behind them.

Soon they heard the clatter of many feet behind them. Looking back, they saw that the stones which Deucalion had thrown had turned into a troop of young men who were following him. The stones that Pyrrha had thrown had become a group of girls who were following her.

Deucalion and Pyrrha were no longer lonely. They had plenty to do. They taught the youths and the maidens the arts of plowing and spinning and weaving that they, themselves, had learned from the gods before the flood.

Stones lay thick on the face of the land, and the valleys were covered with forests. With the stones walls were made, and with timber from the forest, wood floors were laid. Thus, houses were built. Farms were then laid out, fields were sown, and vines and olive trees planted. Soon the valley below Mount Parnassus was crowded with many people. In time the race of Deucalion and Pyrrha spread from valley to valley, up and down the land of Greece.

The people called themselves Hel-le´nes, because one of the sons of Deucalion was named Hel´len. Their country, which we call Greece, they called Hel´las.

Chapter II

CADMUS AND THE DRAGON'S TEETH

In a land of Asia, named Phoe-ni´ci-a, lived King Ag´e-nor with his queen. They had four children — three sons and a beautiful daughter named Eu-ro´pa.

One morning, as the young people were playing in a meadow near the seashore, a snow white bull came toward them. Europa and her brothers thought it would be a fine frolic to take a ride on the back of the bull. The brothers agreed that Europa should have the first ride. In a moment she was on the bull's back, and the bull was capering over the meadow. Then, suddenly, he ran down to the shore and plunged into the sea. For a little while he could be seen swimming through the water with Europa clinging to his horns. Then both disappeared, and Europa never saw her brothers or her father or mother again. Still, her fate was not a sad one. At the end of a long ride on the back of the bull, she reached that part of the world which to this day is called Europe in her honor. There she married a king, and was a queen for the rest of her life.

But in her old home there was great distress. Agenor sent his sons to look for her and told them not to return until they had found their sister. Their mother went with them. After a long time the two elder sons gave up the search and settled in a strange land. The mother and the youngest son, Cad´mus, wandered on until her death. With her last breath she made him promise to go to Mount Parnassus and ask the oracle where he might find Europa. As soon as she was dead, Cadmus made haste to Parnassus. When he arrived at the mountain, he found the cleft in the rocks from which the oracle had once come to Deucalion. Cadmus stood before the stream of gas which poured from it and asked for advice.

Europa on the bulls back

From the cleft came a deep roaring sound. Then he heard the puzzling words, "Follow the cow; and build a city where she lies down."

Cadmus saw a cow nibbling tufts of grass by the roadside, not far from where he was standing. He decided to follow her and, with some companions, set out on his unknown journey.

For a long time it seemed as though the cow would not lie down at all. Finally, she began to double her knees under her, as cows do, and in a second more she was at rest on the ground. Cadmus and his men decided to camp on the spot for the night. They looked about for some water and found a spring bubbling out from under a rock.

Now this was really an enchanted spring. It was guarded by a dragon that had the claws of a lion, the wings of an eagle, and the jaws of a serpent. When Cadmus and his men came near, the dragon sprang from behind the rock and killed all but Cadmus.

Luckily, Cadmus had his sword with him. When the dragon, with wide-open jaws, flew at him, he thrust his sword down the fiery throat and into the creature's heart. The monster fell dead. Through the air rang the words, "Sow the teeth of the dragon, O Cadmus!"

Though he saw that it would be hard work to break the great teeth out of the dragon's jaws, Cadmus at once set about the task. When it was finished, he dug the soil with the point of his sword as best he could and planted half of the monster's teeth.

Never had grown such a wonderful crop. For every tooth that was planted, a warrior, armed and eager to fight, sprang up. Cadmus gazed in amazement, until a voice in the air commanded, "Throw a stone among the warriors."

Cadmus obeyed, and immediately every warrior drew his sword and attacked one of his companions. The woods rang with the din of the battle. One by one the warriors fell, until only five were left. Cadmus now shouted loudly to them, "Be at peace!" When they stopped fighting, he added, "Building is better than killing."

"Then let us build a city here!" cried Cadmus; for they were standing where the cow had lain down.

The warriors agreed, and all set to work to build a city. They called the city Thebes, and in later days it became very famous.

The land around Thebes was rich and covered with grass. So Cadmus and his friends raised cattle. But there were many robbers in Greece who often made raids upon the cattle and stole some of the finest animals.

For protection against the robbers, a wall was built. It was not a wall laid by masons, but a magic wall built by a strange musician called Am´phi-on. He struck such sweet music from his lyre that the stones danced about and took their proper places in the wall.

When Cadmus was a boy at his father's palace in Phoenicia, he and his brothers and the lost Europa had been taught to read and write. Now that peace and plenty filled his land, he determined to teach his people the arts of reading and writing. So the men of Thebes learned their a-b-c's, and Cadmus' school was the first in Europe where people were taught to read.

But Cadmus was not happy. He was condemned to eight years of punishment for killing the dragon. After the punishment was over, Jupiter gave him Harmony, the daughter of Venus, for a wife, and all the gods came to the wedding feast. One of the wedding presents was a necklace that brought bad luck to anyone who wore it. Harmony had great misfortunes. Bowed with grief, she and Cadmus left Thebes and settled in the western part of Greece. Finally, Jupiter pitied them in their trouble, turned them into serpents, and carried them to the realm of the blessed.

Chapter III

PERSEUS

Part I

In a Grecian city named Ar´gos lived beautiful Da-na´e, the king's daughter. An oracle warned the king that he would be killed by Danae's son. To save his life, he ordered Danae and her child, Per´se-us, to be shut up in a chest and cast adrift on the Mediterranean Sea.

For two days and nights the chest floated on the water. At the end of that time it struck against some rocks on the shore of an island called Se´ri-phos. There was a little opening in the side of the chest, and peeping through it, Danae saw a man coming over the rocks toward her. As soon as he was near enough, he threw a fishing net over the chest and drew it ashore.

He broke the chest open and let Danae out. Then he told her that she had landed upon an island ruled by his brother, Pol´y-dec´tes. His own name was Dic´tys. He took Danae and her child to his home.

Years went by, and Perseus grew to be a strong and handsome man. Danae was still a beautiful woman and Polydectes fell in love with her. She refused his love, and Perseus was unwilling that he should marry her. Then Polydectes told Perseus that he was about to marry, and that he wished to give the head of the Gor´gon, Me-du´sa, to his bride for a present. Perseus promised to get him the Gorgon's head. This pleased Polydectes. He did not want the Gorgon's head, but he asked for it because he believed that the young man would never return alive if he went in search of it.

The Gorgons were three horrible sisters who lived on a distant island near the land of the setting sun. Their hair was snakes that hissed at all who came near them. They had wings of gold and claws of brass. Two of them were immortal, but the youngest, Medusa, was mortal. Her face was that of a beautiful woman, but never free from a frown. Whoever looked upon it was turned to stone.

Perseus and the Gray Sisters

When Perseus had made his promise, he went out from the palace and sat on the cliffs of Seriphos. While he was gazing at the white-capped sea, Hermes, the messenger of the gods, appeared before him and promised help from himself and from Athena, the goddess of wisdom. Athena would lend her shield, Hermes offered his sword of light, and both agreed to guide him to the land of the setting sun, where the three Gray Sisters lived. These sisters would tell him the way to the home of the Hes-per´i-des. The Hesperides were beautiful nymphs who had three magic treasures, which Perseus must get before he could reach the land of the Gorgons.

Leaving Seriphos, Perseus began his long journey to the land of the setting sun. When he arrived there he found the three Gray Sisters. They were the strangest beings that he had ever seen. They had among them only one eye and one tooth, which they passed in turn from one to another.

When Perseus reached their dwelling, the door was wide open, and so he walked in. He was overjoyed to find the three sisters all taking a nap, with their one eye and one tooth lying beside them; and he quickly seized both these treasures. That done, he awakened the sisters and inquired of them the way to the home of the Hesperides. At first they refused to tell him, but when they found that he had their eye and tooth, they quickly told him how to go. He then gave them back the eye and the tooth.

It did not take him long to reach the home of the Hesperides. It was an island in the Western Ocean. The nymphs had been told by Athena that he was coming. So when he arrived they gave him welcome and agreed to lend him their magic treasures.

"The distance across the sea to the home of the Gorgons is great," said one of the nymphs to Perseus. "Take therefore these winged sandals of gold. With them you can fly through the air like an eagle."

"The Gorgon's head," said another of the nymphs, "must be kept in this magic wallet, lest you look upon the terrible face and be turned to stone."

"To get near the Gorgons," added the third, "you must wear this cap of darkness, so that you may see without being seen."

The hero then slung the wallet over his shoulder, put the sandals upon his

Above: *Perseus and the Hesperides.*
Right: *Perseus slays the Gorgon and takes her head.*

feet, and the cap upon his head, and vanished. As swift as lightning, he crossed the dark waters and reached the home of the Gorgons. They were all asleep. Without looking at them, Perseus held up the shield of Athena and saw reflected upon it the frowning face of Medusa. With one blow from the sword of Hermes, he struck off her head, and without looking at it, he placed it in his wallet. Then he hurried away from the weird place.

The other Gorgons awoke at once and followed him in furious haste; but as he wore his cap of darkness, they could not see him. With his sandal wings, he flew so fast that he was soon too far for them to follow.

Part II

As he was flying along the coast of Africa, he heard the sound of weeping. He looked down and saw a beautiful girl chained to a rock at the water's edge. Hastening to her, he took off his cap of darkness that she might see him. "Fair maiden," he exclaimed, "why are you chained to this rock?"

"Alas!" she cried. "I have been offered as a sacrifice to Poseidon. You cannot save me, however much you want to."

Her words made Perseus the more determined to help her. "Why is Poseidon angry?" he asked. "And who has dared to treat you so cruelly?"

"I am An-drom´e-da, daughter of Ce´phe-us and Cas´si-o-pe´ia, king and queen of this land," replied the maiden. "My mother boasted that I was more beautiful than any nymph

Perseus rescues Andromeda

in Poseidon's palace. Her pride enraged Poseidon so that he raised great storms and sent a terrible monster to devour our people. The priests said that if I were offered to him, the rest of the people would be spared."

Then with the sword of light Perseus cut the chain which bound Andromeda to the rock. At this moment the monster, huge and ugly, came plowing through the water. Perseus could not be seen because he had put on his cap of darkness. Before the creature could harm the maiden, it's head was cut off by the sword of light.

On his swift-winged sandals, Perseus, with Andromeda in his arms, now flew to the palace of Cepheus and Cassiopeia.

There had been many glad weddings before that of Perseus and Andromeda, but none was ever more joyful. He was admired as a wonderful hero, and everyone loved the girl who had been willing to give her life to save her people.

After the wedding, Perseus went back to Seriphos, taking Andromeda with him. When he reached the island, Polydectes was in his palace feasting. Perseus hastened at once to the banquet hall and said to the king, "See! I have brought that which you desired."

With these words he held up the head of the Gorgon. The king and his courtiers gave one look and were instantly turned to stone.

The Gorgon's head had now done its work; so Perseus carried it to the temple of Athena and there offered it to the goddess. Ever after she wore it upon her shield, and its snaky ringlets and frowning face are to be seen upon her statues. The sword of light was given back to Hermes, who also returned the winged sandals, the magic wallet and the cap of darkness to the Hesperides.

Part III

You will remember that Argos was the birthplace of Perseus, and to that city he now returned, taking Andromeda with him. His grandfather, who was still king of Argos, remembered that the oracle had said that he would die by the hand of Danae's son and was much alarmed. Perseus, however, quieted the fears of the king, and the two became very good friends. But it was while playing quoits one day that Perseus accidentally hit his grandfather with a quoit. The wound caused the king's death. And thus, as the Greeks used to say, "What had been fated came to pass."

Perseus was overwhelmed with sorrow. He could not bear to live any longer at Argos and, therefore, gave his kingdom to a kinsman of his in exchange for the kingdom of Ti´ryns.

At Tiryns he ruled long and wisely. The gods gave him and Andromeda a glorious place among the stars after their deaths. With Cepheus and Cassiopeia they can still be seen in the skies not far from where the Great Bear shines.

Chapter IV

HERCULES AND HIS LABORS

Part I

Greatest of all the heroes of Greece was Her´a-cles, who was born in Thebes, the city of Cadmus. His mother was one of the descendants of Perseus and his father was Zeus. We know him by the name Her´cu-les, for that is what the Romans called him.

Hera, the queen of the gods, hated Hercules. When he was only a baby in the cradle, she sent two large serpents to devour him. He grasped the throat of each serpent with his tiny fingers and choked both to death.

When he had grown to manhood, he was forced by the will of the gods to become a slave of a hard-hearted cousin of his named Eu-rys´the-us, who was king of My-ce´nae.

Eurystheus set twelve tasks for Hercules. The first was to kill the Ne-me´an lion. This was a ferocious animal that lived in the forest of Ne´me-a and ate a child or grown person every two or three days. Its skin was so tough that nothing could pierce it. But Hercules drove the lion before him into a cave and following boldly, grasped the beast about the neck and choked it to death. That done, he stripped off its skin, which he ever after wore as a cloak.

When the Nemean lion had been killed, Eurystheus said to Hercules, "You must now kill the hydra that lives in the marsh of Ler´na."

This hydra was a nine-headed serpent whose very breath was poisonous. It was hard to kill the creature, because as soon as one head was cut off, two others at once sprang up in its place. This task might have proved too much for Hercules if a friend had not prevented new heads from growing by burning each neck with a firebrand the instant that Hercules cut off the head.

The third of Hercules' tasks was to bring to Eurystheus the stag with the golden horns that was sacred to Artemis. It lived in southern Greece in the woods of Ar-ca´di-a. It had brazen feet and could run so fast that Hercules had to chase it for a whole year before he caught it.

"Now," said Eurystheus, "you must kill the boar that roams on the slopes of Mount Er´y-man´thus." This creature laid waste the farmers' fields of barley and wheat at the foot of the mountain. Hercules captured the brute in a net and killed it.

The next command of Eurystheus to Hercules was, "Clean the Au-ge´an stables."

The Augean stables belonged to Au-ge´as, one of the kings of Greece. As three thousand oxen were kept in them, and as they had not been cleaned for thirty years, they were filthy. Hercules cleaned them in one day. He dug a great ditch as far as the stables and turned into it the waters of two swift rivers.

Part II

As soon as this was done, Eurystheus said, "You must now kill the birds of Lake Stym-pha´lus. Instead of wings of feathers, these birds had wings of arrows which darted out and shot anyone who passed by. Their claws and beaks were of brass, and they fed of human flesh. Hercules killed them with poisoned arrows.

Still Eurystheus hoped to find some task that might prove too much for the hero, so he said, "Bring me the bull of Crete."

This bull was a terrible monster that had been sent by Poseidon to ravage Crete, an island not far from Greece. Hercules set out for Crete at once. He conquered the bull, rode on his back across the sea from Crete to Greece, then swung the great animal to his own shoulders and carried him to Eurystheus.

Eurystheus now said to his wonderful slave, "Tame the man-eating horses of Di´o-me´des, king of Thrace." He fully expected that this task would be fatal to Hercules. But the hero went to the palace of Diomedes and soon discovered a way to tame the savage steeds. He killed Diomedes and threw his flesh to them, and the man-eating beasts became like other horses and gladly ate oats and grass.

Eurystheus immediately set a ninth task.

"My daughter," said he, "wants the girdle of the queen of the Am´a-zons. Get it for her."

The Amazons were a nation living upon the shores of the Black Sea. It was the custom for the women to go to battle. Bravest of them all was Queen Hy-pol´y-te, whom Ares had rewarded for her courage by giving her a beautiful girdle. All Greece had heard of this girdle, and it was no wonder that the daughter of Eurystheus wished to have it.

When Hercules reached the country of the Amazons and made known his errand, he found that the queen was as generous as she was brave. She said that she would send her girdle as a present to the daughter of Eurystheus. So it looked as though Hercules was to have no trouble at all with this task. Hera, however, tried to prevent his success. She made herself look like one of the Amazons and went among them. She persuaded them that Hercules wished to carry away their queen. A great quarrel then arose between the hero and the Amazons, which ended in a battle. Brave Hipolyte was killed, and Hercules then took the girdle and carried it to Eurystheus.

Part III

"Bring me the oxen of Ge´ry-on," Eurystheus now commanded.

Geryon was a monster with three bodies. He lived on an island in the Western Ocean, as the Greeks called the Atlantic Ocean. In the fields of this island grazed Geryon's herd of red oxen, guarded by a two-headed dog. At first Hercules did not see how he could reach the island. But Apollo, the god of the sun, came to his aid and said to him, "I will lend you the golden bowl in which I sail every night from the land of the Western Sea to the land of the rising sun."

So in the sun's golden bowl Hercules reached the island safely. He slew the two-headed dog, then got the whole herd of oxen into the golden bowl and sailed back.

For the tenth time Eurystheus was amazed. He now commanded Hercules, "Get me some of the apples of the Hesperides."

At the wedding of Zeus and Hera, the grandest that ever took place on Olympus, Demeter, the great earth-mother, had given to Hera some branches loaded with golden apples. These branches were afterwards planted and grew into trees upon islands in the Western Ocean, far away from Greece. The trees and their fruit were guarded by three nymphs called the Hersperides, who were aided by a terrible dragon. When Hercules was told to get some of the apples of the Hesperides, he was puzzled. At last he went to Atlas, who was the father of the Hesperides, and begged his help. Atlas lived in Africa, opposite

Spain. His duty was to hold up the sky, with all it contains — the sun, moon and stars.

"I will get you some of the apples," said Atlas in answer to Hercules, "if you will hold up the sky for me while I am getting them."

The bargain was made. Hercules held up the sky while Atlas went and secured three of the golden apples. Then the giant took the sky again on his shoulders, and Hercules carried the apples to Eurystheus.

The Fates allowed Eurystheus to send Hercules upon only one more of his dangerous errands.

"Go to gates of the underworld," said Eurystheus, "and bring Cerberus here."

Hercules now, if ever, had need of aid from the gods. They did not fail him. Mercury, the god who guided the souls of the dead to the unseen world, and Athena, the goddess of wisdom, both went with him to the kingdom of Hades.

Hades said that if Hercules could overpower Cerberus without using any weapon, he might take the great watchdog to the world of light. Hercules wrestled with the monster, overcame him, and dragged him to the palace of Eurystheus.

This ended the power of Eurystheus over the hero.

Part IV

Hercules had a friend named Ad-me´tus, a king in Thes´sa-ly, who was about to die. The Fates had promised that his life should be spared if his father, mother or wife would die for him. When both father and mother refused, Al-ces´tis, his wife, gave her life for him. Admetus was crazed with grief at losing her, and so Hercules went to Hades' kingdom, seized Alcestis, and brought her to her husband.

Hercules was forced to become a slave to Omphale, who dressed him as a woman and made him kneel at her feet, spin thread, and do a woman's work for three years.

Once Hercules became insane and killed a friend whom he greatly loved. The gods punished him for this with a serious sickness. He asked Apollo to cure him, but the god refused, and Hercules tried to carry away the tripod on which the priestess of Delphi sat when the god spoke to her. For this he was deprived of his great strength and given as a slave to Om-pha´le, Queen of Lydia. She took the

Nemean lion's skin from him and dressed him as a woman. Then she made him kneel at her feet, spin thread, and do a woman's work for three years. After he was again free he did many brave deeds.

Once when journeying with his wife Deianira, he reached a river. There was neither bridge nor ferry. Nes´sus, the centaur — half-man, half-horse — who

Nessus carrying off Deianira

owned that part of the river, undertook to carry Deianira across while Hercules waded. When Nessus reached the middle of the river he tried to run away with Deianira, but Hercules shot him with one of his poisoned arrows. Nessus, while dying, told Deianira to save some of his blood and use it as a charm to make Hercules love her more.

Part V

Some years after this, Deianira became very jealous, and the foolish woman sprinkled some drops of the centaur's poisoned blood upon a robe that Hercules had to wear at a sacrifice. When Hercules put on the robe the poison burned like fire. He tried to pull off the garment, but it clung to him and, as he pulled it, his flesh was torn.

Seeing now that his end was near, he went to the top of a mountain. There he pulled up some trees by the roots and heaped them together to make his funeral pyre. With his club for a pillow and his lion skin for a cover, he lay upon the pyre and soon he ceased to breathe. A friend kindled the pyre, and the hero's body was burned to ashes. Then a cloud, gleaming as though on fire, descended through the air, and amid the pealing of thunder the mighty spirit was borne to the skies.

There Zeus made him one of the gods and gave him the beautiful goddess Hebe for a wife.

Map of Anceint Greece and surrounding nations

Chapter V

JASON AND THE GOLDEN FLEECE

Part I

In a city of Greece named I-ol´cus a good man called Ae´son was king. His younger brother, Pe´li-as, seized the throne. But Pelias did not enjoy much happiness in his stolen kingdom. He had no fear of Aeson, who was a weak man. But he was very much afraid that Aeson's son Ja´son, then only a boy, might someday take the kingdom from him.

So he tried to kill Jason, but the child was taken away by night and Pelias never found him. It was said that he was dead. Twenty years passed. Though Jason was never seen in Iolcus, Pelias was still afraid that he was alive. Finally, to settle the matter, he consulted the oracle of Apollo.

He received the answer, "Beware of the man who wears but one sandal."

After that Pelias ordered the watchman at the city gate to take notice of the feet of every stranger who entered the city.

Jason had been all these years in the charge of Chi´ron, the centaur, who was the most famous teacher in Greece. Jason had heard of the wickedness of his uncle. Now that he was a man, he determined to regain his father's kingdom.

So one day he set out for Iolcus. On the way he came to a wide stream over which there was no bridge. At the same time a feeble old woman came up and wished to cross. The stream was swollen, and it looked as if she would be swept away by the current and

Jason comes to the aid of Hera

Greek Sandals

drowned if she tried to wade across. So Jason took her in his arms and carried her over. But that woman was really Hera, the Queen of the gods. She had come down from Olympus to take a journey on earth without telling anyone who she was, because she wished to find out if there was any real kindness among men. She never forgot Jason's courtesy. He owed his success in his career to her help.

In crossing the stream he lost one of his sandals, and so he reached Iolcus with one foot bare. He cared very little about this; but when word was brought to Pelias that a man wearing one sandal had entered the city, the king was greatly alarmed.

"Either I must kill that man," Pelias said to himself, "or he will kill me." He therefore sent a messenger to invite the stranger to the palace, and Jason soon stood before him.

"What would you do," asked Pelias, "if you had in your power the man who was fated to kill you?"

"I should tell him," answered Jason, "to go to Col´chis and bring me the Golden Fleece."

"Then you shall go," cried Pelias. "You have come to take my kingdom from me; but not till you bring me that fleece will I yield you my crown."

The story of the Golden Fleece is very interesting.

Many years before, one of the Grecian kings, who had a son named Phrix´us, was told by an oracle that Zeus wished him to offer up his son as a sacrifice. The poor father prepared to make the offering. As the young man was standing before the altar and his father was just about to slay him, a ram with shining fleece of gold came down from the sky and stood beside them. Phrixus jumped to the back of the ram. His sister, Hel´le, who was standing with him at the altar, jumped on behind her brother, and the ram immediately ran off with the two. He went so fast that people who saw him thought he had wings. When he came to the strait that separates Europe from Asia, he plunged into the waves. Poor Helle soon fell off and was drowned. After that the strait was called by the Greeks the Hel´les-pont, a word that means the Sea of Helle. It is the strait that is named the Dar´da-nelles on our maps.

The ram carried Phrixus safely across the strait, and went on until he reached the palace of Ae-e´tes, the king of a country of Col´chis, which lay on the shores of the Black Sea.

Phrixus felt very thankful for having made such a journey in safety, so he offered the ram as a sacrifice to Zeus and nailed the Fleece to a tree that was sacred to Ares.

This Fleece became one of the wonders of the world. Lest it should be stolen, a dragon was set to watch it. Many persons tried to get possession of it, but most, if not all of them, lost their lives in the attempt.

Jason knew all this, but he said at once that he would get the Fleece. Before setting out on the journey, however, he went to a place called Do-do´na to ask the advice of Zeus. At Dodona there was a wonderful talking oak which told men the advice and commands of Zeus. As soon as Jason came near the oak the leaves began to rustle, and a voice from within the tree said, "Build a fifty-oared ship. Take as companions the greatest heroes of Greece. Cut a branch from the talking oak and make it a part of the prow of the vessel."

All these commands Jason obeyed. The ship was built and a piece of the talking oak was used in making her prow. Jason invited forty-nine of the bravest men of Greece to go on the expedition. He named his ship the Argo, and he and his companions are known as the Ar´go-nauts, or sailors on the Argo. One of them was Or´phe-us, the greatest musician that ever played or sang in Greece. It was said of him that the trees of a forest once danced in wild delight at his music.

This wonderful musician was of very great use on the Argo. The ship was the largest that had ever been built in Greece, and it was found too heavy to launch. The strength of all the fifty heroes did not move it an inch. Jason did not know what to do. He consulted the talking prow, which told him that everybody must get on board and that Orpheus must then play his lyre and sing. No sooner was the music heard than the great ship glided easily into the water. The famous voyage began.

Another companion of Jason was Hercules, about whose wonderful labors you have read. Then there were Cas´tor and Pol´lux, twin brothers, who did such wonders that after their death, the gods took them to heaven. There they still shine as stars in the constellation called the "Twins."

Still another of the Argonauts was a hero named Lyn´ceus, which means the lynx-eyed. He was kept on watch all through the Argo's voyage, because he could see a whole day's trip ahead.

Part II

After many adventures, the Argonauts at last reached the Black Sea and the shores of Colchis. Aetes received them in a kind manner, but he was not at all pleased when he learned their errand. There was nothing in his kingdom which he prized as much as he prized the Golden Fleece.

However, when Jason explained the matter, Aetes said, "Very well, you may try to get the Fleece if you choose to run the risk. But first you must yoke my pair of brazen-footed, fire-breathing bulls, and use them to plow a field near the grove where the Golden Fleece hangs. After you have done this, you must sow the field with some of the teeth of the dragon that Cadmus killed. Finally, you must fight with the dragon that guards the Fleece."

Medea mixing a potion

Aetes felt sure that Jason would lose his life in trying to do all this. Many brave men had been burned to death in the streams of fire that the bulls breathed out of their nostrils.

King Aetes had a daughter named Me-de´a. She was famed for her beauty and her skill as an enchantress. Fortunately, she fell in love with Jason and came to his aid.

"Take this ointment," said Medea, "and rub it all over your body. Then the flaming breath of the bulls cannot harm you. At midnight I will go with you to the pasture where the creatures feed."

That night Jason went with Medea and found the bulls in the pasture. The magic ointment saved him from being burned by their fiery breath. He seized and yoked them without any trouble, and very soon, the field was plowed and harrowed. Jason sowed the teeth of the dragon and then stood waiting to see what would happen.

Soon points of light glistened here and there in the soil. They were the tops of helmets coming up out of the ground and touched by the rays of the rising sun. In no great while where each point of light had appeared, there stood a full-armed warrior.

"Throw a stone into the midst of the host!" Medea commanded. Jason obeyed.

The stone struck one warrior, glanced off to another and then to a third. The new-born heroes, not knowing where the stone had come from, became wild with rage. They hacked and battered one another with swords and clubs until only one of them was left. He was fatally wounded.

Then Jason went back to the palace and told Aetes what he had done. He said that he was ready to fight the dragon that guarded the Golden Fleece.

At midnight he went with Medea to the grove in which the Fleece hung. The dragon rushed with wide-open jaws to devour him, but Medea threw an enchanted potion into the monster's mouth, and he sank to the ground in a death-like sleep.

"Make haste!" cried Medea. "Take down the Fleece." In a twinkling Jason had done so. "Now," she added, "we must start at once for Greece. My father will never really let you carry the Fleece from Colchis."

Taking Medea with him, Jason made all haste to the Argo. When he reached the shore where the ship lay, his companions welcomed him heartily. They were filled with delight when they saw the Golden Fleece. All hurried on board the Argo, the sails were hoisted, and the ship began her homeward voyage.

To get back to Greece, the Argonauts had to sail past the Isle of the Si´rens. The Sirens were maidens with beautiful faces but cruel hearts. They sat upon dangerous rocks on the shore of their island and sang songs of enchanting sweetness. Sailors who heard them would steer nearer and nearer, until their vessels were wrecked on the jagged rocks. The Argonauts escaped this peril through the help of Orpheus. He played his lyre and sang more sweetly than even the Sirens. By listening to him, Jason and his companions steered their vessel beyond the dangerous rocks.

As soon as Jason reached Iolchus again, he showed the Golden Fleece to Pelias, and then hung it up as a thank offering in the temple of one of the gods. What became of it after that, nobody knows.

While Jason was getting the Golden Fleece, Pelias had Aeson murdered. In revenge, Medea plotted to have Pelias killed by his own daughters. After Pelias was killed, one of his sons drove Jason and Medea from Iolchus.

Chapter VI

THESEUS

Part I

One of the most violent quarrels that ever disturbed the life of the gods was between Poseidon and Athena.

Ce´crops, one of the wisest of the Greeks, was founding a city near the finest harbor in Greece. Poseidon wished to be the chief god of the city, and Athena also desired the honor.

Poseidon said that as the city was going to be a great seaport — busy with vessels sailing in and sailing out — it was only right that he, the god of the ocean, should be its guardian. Athena foresaw that in days to come the men of the city would care much less about commerce than about art and learning. She thought that she, the goddess of wisdom, should be its guardian.

The other gods became very weary of the quarrel, and to bring it to an end, Jupiter ordered that the one who should offer the more useful gift to the city should become its chief god.

Then with his trident, Poseidon struck a rock within the city's bounds, and up sprang a war horse ready for battle. Athena touched the earth, and an olive tree rose on the spot.

Now groves of olive trees, Jupiter knew well, would be far more useful to the people than the finest of war horses. He therefore decided in favor of Athena. The city became the most famous place in all the world for learning and art, and from Athena, the name of the goddess, it was called Athens.

Part II

The most noted of the early kings of Athens was The´seus, the son of Ae´geus, who was himself a king of Athens. Theseus was born far away from Athens and was brought up by his mother, Ae´thra, at the home of her father.

Before parting with Aethra at her father's home, Aegeus placed a sword and a pair of sandals under a heavy stone and said to her, "When the child is able to lift that stone, let him take the sandals and sword and come to me."

Years went by, and when Theseus had grown up, his mother led him one day to the stone and said to him, "If you are a man, lift that stone."

Theseus lifted it with ease and saw a pair of sandals and a sword.

His mother told him that the sandals and the sword had been placed under the stone by his father, Aegeus, who was king of Athens. "Put them on and seek him in Athens," she said.

He fastened the sword to his girdle and buckled the sandals on his feet. Then he kissed his mother and set out for Athens.

He did not go far without an adventure. A robber called the Club-bearer attacked him. A struggle followed, and the Club-bearer was killed. Then Theseus took the robber's club and ever after that carried it himself.

A little farther on he met a robber called Si´nis, who was known as the Pine-bender. It was the Pine-bender's sport to pull down pine trees, tie travelers to their tops, and let the trees spring back. His victims dangled from the tree tops until they perished from pain and hunger. When Theseus came along he bent a pine, fastened the Pine-bender to it, let the tree spring back, and left the robber to suffer the same torture he had inflicted on so many others.

Journeying still farther, the hero reached the dwelling of Pro-crus´tes, the Stretcher. Procrustes had a bed which he made all travelers fit. If a man's legs were too long, Procrustes cut them to the right length. If they were too short, he stretched them until they were long enough. Theseus forced Procrustes to lie upon the bed himself and chopped the Stretcher's legs to the right length.

In this manner, fighting often and bravely, Theseus made his way to Athens. When he reached the city and showed his sword to Aegeus, the king knew that the young man must be his son. He was filled with joy and declared Theseus his heir.

Part III

Every year the city of Athens had to send seven young men and seven maidens to Mi´nos, the king of Crete, to be devoured by a terrible creature, called the Min´o-taur. It was kept in a place known as the Lab´y-rinth. The Labyrinth was full of winding paths so puzzling that a person, once in, could not find his way out.

The day that the youths and maidens were to sail to Crete was at hand, and Athens was filled with sorrow. Theseus made up his mind that never again should the city have cause for such grief. He determined to kill the Minotaur.

"Father," he said to Aegeus, "let me go to Crete as one of the victims."

"No, no, my son!" cried Aegeus, "I could not bear to lose you."

"Ah, but you will not lose me," answered Theseus. "Not only shall I return, but I will bring back in safety all who go with me."

Victims of the Minotaur

Aegeus at last gave consent and Theseus went as one of the fourteen victims.

The ship's sail was black, an emblem of mourning. As Theseus bade farewell to his father, he said, "I am taking a white sail with me to hoist when we come back. If the black sail should still be set when the ship comes home, you will know that I have failed. But I shall not fail."

The Minotaur

When the black-sailed vessel reached the shores of Crete, there was a great crowd gathered to see the victims. Among the watchers was A´ri-ad´ne, the lovely daughter of the king of Crete. She was full of pity for those who were to be devoured. When she was told that Theseus had determined to fight the Minotaur, she made up her mind to help him. She could see that he was very strong and she felt sure that he could kill the monster. But she feared that he would starve to death in the Labyrinth because he would not be able to find his way out. So when Theseus went into the Labyrinth, she gave him the end of a ball of thread and said, "I will stand here at the entrance and let the ball unwind as you go in. When you have killed the Minotaur, follow the thread back to me."

So Theseus took hold of the thread and went boldly into the Labyrinth. When he reached the center of it, the monster came to attack him. Its weapons were stones. Stone after stone was flung by the monster, but each was warded off by Theseus just as a skillful batter wards off a swift ball. At length, Theseus was close enough to strike the Minotaur with his sword, and the creature fell dead.

Guided by the thread, Theseus quickly made his way back to the entrance of the

Ariadne

Labyrinth. There he was joyfully received by Ariadne and the youths and maidens whom he had saved from death.

Theseus and Ariadne had fallen in love with each other, and when the tribute ship set sail for Greece, Ariadne was one of the passengers.

On the homeward voyage the ship touched at the island of Nax´os. There Theseus had a strange dream. In it he was told by Athena to leave Ariadne on the island, because the Fates intended her to be the wife of one of the gods.

Accordingly, he left her on the island of Naxos and sailed away to Greece. She afterwards did become the bride of one of the gods who gave her a golden crown. After her death, the crown was changed to a crown of stars that is still to be seen in the sky on any bright night.

On the voyage from the island of Naxos to Athens, Theseus was thinking so much about Ariadne that he quite forgot to change the black sail for the white one. This was an unfortunate oversight, for it brought death to Aegeus and sorrow to Theseus.

Day after day, while Theseus was away, Aegeus had sat on a cliff which overlooked the sea, hoping to catch sight of the white sail. When at last the ship appeared with its black sail still spread, the poor king supposed that his son had been devoured by the Minotaur. He threw up his hands in grief, and falling down from the cliff into the sea, was drowned. From that day to this the sea has been called the Ae-ge´an, or the Sea of Aegeus.

When the ship reached the harbor of Athens, Theseus learned of his father's death, and bitterly did he mourn that he had forgotten to hoist the white sail.

He at once became king. No king ever did more for Athens than he. Yet in spite of his love and labor for the city, the Athenians were not grateful. After a while he went on a journey. He remained away so long that they chose a new king in his place. When at last he came back and found that the people whom he had loved so well had forgotten him, he left the city and soon died.

In later days, the Athenians repented that they had been so ungrateful. They brought his bones to Athens and buried them with great solemnity. Festivals were held in his honor, and he was ranked almost with Athena herself as a guardian of the beautiful city.

The story is told that centuries after his death, he left the spirit world and helped the Athenians to gain the victory in the greatest battle they ever fought, the battle of Mar´a-thon, of which you will read further on in this book.

Chapter VII

AGAMEMNON, KING OF MEN

Heroes of the Trojan War

The early kings of Mycenae were thought to be descendants of Zeus. One of these, named Ag´a-mem´non, was the most powerful king in Greece in his day, and thus he was called the "King of Men." During his reign the famous Trojan War occurred. It was supposed to have taken place about 1200 years before the birth of Christ. All of the most famous heroes in Greece took part in it. The story of the events that brought it on is full of interest.

A wonderful wedding took place in Greece. Pe´leus, the brave king of Thessaly, married the beautiful sea-nymph, The´tis. The wedding feast was held on Mount Pe´li-on near the home of the gods. To show their love for Thetis, all the gods came down from Olympus. Apollo shot sunbeams through the quivering oak leaves, and the floor of the forest was dappled with golden light. Nymphs had hung garlands of snow white roses from tree to tree. Wild vines were covered with blossoms, and the air was filled with their fragrance.

But while the Muses were singing their sweetest songs, a golden apple suddenly fell among the gods and goddesses. It had been thrown by the goddess of discord, who was angry because she had not been asked to the wedding.

Hermes, who of course was among the guests, picked up the apple and read the words written upon it to the wedding party. He read, "Let the most beautiful have me."

Hera, Athena, and Aphrodite each claimed that the apple was hers. The quarrel of the god-

37

Paris presents the golden apple to Aphrodite

desses ended only when Zeus said to them, "Go with Hermes over the sea to Mount Ida, and let Par´is, the shepherd, decide the matter."

At once the goddesses, led by Hermes, sped through the air to Mount Ida to find Paris.

Paris was the son of Pri´am, the king of a rich and powerful city called Troy, which was opposite Greece on the shore of the Aegean Sea. His mother dreamed that he would one day set Troy on fire. Because of this, as soon as he was born, King Priam ordered one of his shepherds to carry the infant to the snow-capped Mount Ida, near Troy, and leave him there to die of cold and hunger.

Five days after leaving the child, the shepherd found it still alive. This made him think that the gods did not wish him to die; so he carried Paris home to his wife. They brought him up as their own child.

Paris thought himself only a shepherd's boy and tended King Priam's herds while they grazed on the slopes of Mount Ida.

On the day of the wedding upon Mount Pelion, as he sat watching the flock, Hermes and his three companions suddenly appeared before him. The goddesses were all so lovely that when they asked Paris to say which was the most beautiful, he was greatly perplexed. Each tried to persuade him to decide in her favor. Hera promised to make him the greatest of kings. Athena said that she would make him the wisest of men. Aphrodite declared that she would give him the most beautiful woman in the world as his wife. He awarded the apple to Aphrodite, but by doing so, he greatly offended Athena and Hera.

Not long after this, Paris went to Troy and took part in some games that were held at the court of Priam. These games involved wrestling, boxing, and running races. The unknown shepherd carried off many prizes. It was soon found out who he really was, and Priam heartily welcomed him home.

Meantime, Aphrodite had not forgotten her promise. She advised Paris to sail to Greece, where he would find the most beautiful woman in the world. This was Helen, the wife of Men´e-la´us, king of Sparta. Paris went to Sparta and with the help of Aphrodite, won the heart of Helen and took her away with him to Troy.

When Menelaus found that his wife had been stolen, he sent a message to the kings of all the states of Greece. He asked them to help him regain Helen and punish Paris. Now thirty or more of the kings had wished to marry Helen before she had chosen Menelaus as her husband. All these men had sworn to aid the one chosen if anyone should ever try to take her away from the man she chose to marry. As soon as they received the message from Menelaus, the kings began to make ready for war against the Trojans in accordance with their oath.

Meanwhile, Menelaus' brother, Agamemnon, was busy preparing for war. His woodsmen were cutting yew trees for the making of bows and gathering reeds for the making of arrows. His smiths were making swords and spearheads and javelins. In his shipyards hundreds of men were building ships. The roads were alive with countrymen bringing in loads of wheat, barley, bacon, and olives to store in the vessels.

At last one hundred black ships were ready, and Agamemnon set sail. A place named Au´lis had been selected where the Greeks were to meet. Twelve hundred ships assembled there, and Agamemnon was chosen commander-in-chief.

Just as the ships were about to start for Troy, a terrible storm came up. Agamemnon felt sure that one of the gods must be angry with the Greeks. He consulted a soothsayer named Cal´chas. "Artemis is angry, great King," said Calchas, "but not with the Greeks. Thou hast slain a deer in the forest and boasted that thou hast greater skill in the chase than Artemis, herself. Never, O King," he added, "can the storm be lulled until thou hast offered thy daughter Iph´i-ge-ni´a as a sacrifice on the altar of Artemis."

Agamemnon was heart broken, but he felt that the will of Artemis must be done. He sent a messenger to the mother of Iphigenia to say that A-chil´les, a Greek prince, wished to marry the girl, and that she must come to Aulis at once. This was only a device to get Iphigenia to Aulis.

However, when she reached Aulis and heard the truth from her father, the girl behaved nobly. "My father," she said, "if my death will help the Greeks, I am ready to die."

Her words sent a thrill through all the host and ninety thousand brave men sorrowed. Achilles and A´jax, sternest of warriors, wept, and Agamemnon was wild with grief.

While the girl was lying upon the altar, and the priestess of Artemis was standing near,

The sacrifice of Iphigenia

the goddess, watching from Olympus, was moved to pity. Just as the father had lifted his sword to slay the girl, a cloud as bright as shining snow appeared above him. Artemis stepped from the cloud, lifted the girl from the altar, and carried her through the air to one of her temples, where she made her a priestess. On the altar lay a white fawn which was sacrificed instead of Iphigenia.

And now the fairest winds blew, the sails of the Grecian ships were set, the fleet sailed swiftly to Troy, and the siege of that city began.

Chapter VIII

ACHILLES, BRAVEST OF GREEKS

Bravest of all the Greeks who went to fight the Trojans was Achilles. He was said to be the son of Peleus and the beautiful sea nymph Thetis, at whose marriage feast the goddess of discord had thrown the golden apple among the guests.

Thetis, herself, could never die, and when Achilles was born, she was determined to make him immortal also. With the child in her arms, she went down to the gloomy kingdom of Hades. You will remember that a dark river called the Styx flowed round the underworld. If a mortal were dipped into the Styx, no sword or arrow or other weapon could injure him. Thetis held Achilles by the heel and dipped him into the water. In her haste to get out of the underworld, she forgot to dip in the heel by which she had held the child. So in that heel, and only there, Achilles could be wounded.

When Thetis heard that the Greeks were going to fight the Trojans, she was greatly distressed. She knew that if her son went to the war, he would certainly lose his life. She dressed him as a girl and took him to Scy′ros, a far away island of Greece, and left him there in the palace of the king, Lyc′o-me′des.

Now Calchis had foretold that Troy could never be taken without the help of Achilles. The Greek princes were determined that he should go with them.

A Grecian chief, called O-dys′se-us the Crafty, learned where he was hidden and set out to find him. This chief is more often referred to today by his Roman name, U-lys′ses.

One day a peddler appeared at the gate of the palace in Scyros, bringing all sorts of beautiful things for sale. The princesses were wild with delight as the peddler showed them one thing after another. Suddenly, the blast of a war trumpet rang through the air. All but one girl ran away. That girl seized a shield and a spear which were among the peddler's wares and stood, instantly ready for battle.

Then the peddler, who was really Odysseus, knew that he had found Achilles. Odysseus told the young man that all the princes of the Greeks were preparing for war against Troy. Achilles was eager to go with them, and so in spite of all that Thetis had done, her son sailed to Troy with the other Greek princes. For nine years he was the champion of the Greeks.

In the tenth year of the war a great misfortune befell the Greeks. They had taken two beautiful maidens captive. One of the maidens had been given as a slave to Achilles, the other to Agamemnon. Now it happened that Agamemnon's slave was the daughter of Chry´ses, a priest of the sun god Apollo.

The loss of his daughter was a great grief to Chryses, and he prayed to Apollo for vengeance. In answer, Apollo drew his bow and shot arrows which brought terrible pestilence into the camp of the Greeks. The tents were soon filled with the dead and dying.

The soothsayer Calchas, told the Greeks why Apollo had punished them, and the girl was sent back to her father. The god was satisfied, and his arrows stopped bringing the plague to the Greeks.

But Agamemnon now took the other maiden from Achilles, and this made the son of Thetis so angry that he declared he would help the Greeks no more. For days and days he stayed in his tent, or sat by the seashore and told his wrongs to his mother.

Then the Trojans, learning that Achilles was not fighting, grew bold and at last came out through the gates of their city and drove the Greeks from the field. Hector, a son of Priam, followed them to their ships. Some of the Trojans took lighted torches and tried to burn the Greek fleet. One ship caught fire. Just then, however, there rushed to the shore a warrior who looked so like Achilles that the Trojans fled from the ships to the gates of their city. The unknown warrior was not Achilles, but Pa-tro´clus, his devoted friend, who had put

The Trojans attempt to burn the Greek fleet.

Above: *Achilles with the body of Hector*
Right: *Thetis with the armor for Achilles*

on Achilles' armor. The Trojans had mistaken him for the great hero. Even Hector fled before him. But Apollo, who fought on the side of the Trojans, at last shot an arrow from his silver bow. The arrow struck Patroclus, and he fell to the earth. Hector then slew him and carried off Achilles' armor as his prize.

When Achilles learned that his friend had been killed, he forgot his anger and rushed from the tent shouting the war cry of the Greeks. He had neither shield nor spear. Yet the Trojans fled at the sound of his voice. The ships and tents of the Greeks were saved.

The body of Patroclus was then carried into the tent of Achilles, and the hero wept for his friend.

As he sat mourning, his mother Thetis rose from her home in the sea and came to comfort him. She then went to Hephaestus, the great blacksmith, who you remember, made all things of iron and bronze for the gods and said, "Good Hephaestus, make for my son such a suit of armor as never mortal has worn."

Soon the forges of Aetna were glowing. The Cyclops' anvils were ringing, and a suit of armor fit for a god was made. In this armor Achilles made terrible havoc among the Trojans. He scattered them as a wolf might scatter a flock of sheep. He killed Hector at last, tied the

The Trojan Horse

body to his chariot, and dragged it three times round the tomb of Patroclus.

Paris avenged the death of Hector by wounding Achilles in the heel. From the wound the great hero died.

Hundreds of Trojans had been killed by the Greeks, but the walls of Troy still stood, and not one Grecian warrior had entered the gates.

Troy was kept safe in a wonderful way. In the city was an image of Athena which the Trojans believed had come down from heaven. It was called the Pal-la´di-um, from Pal´las, another name for Athena. So long as the Palladium stood in its place, Troy could never be captured.

At length, crafty Odysseus, with the help of another Greek warrior named Di´o-me´des, got possession of the Palladium. One night the two climbed the walls of Troy, went to the temple where the Palladium was kept, and carried the image away.

When they returned to the Grecian camp, Odysseus advised the Greeks to build a huge wooden horse. When it was finished it was filled with armed men and left standing before the walls of the city. Then the Grecian army burned their tents and sailed away as if they were going home. But really, they only went a short distance and hid behind an island not far from the Trojan coast.

One Greek named Si´non had been left behind. He told the Trojans that the wooden horse would protect their city, just as the Palladium had done. So, very foolishly, they drew the horse within the walls.

When night came Sinon released the armed men from the horse and signalled to the Greek fleet with a flaming torch. In a very short time the ships were all back and the Greek soldiers again were swarming before the walls of Troy. The city gates were opened by Sinon and his companions, and in poured the Greeks by the thousands. They slaughtered the sleeping Trojans, sacked the palace of Priam, and burned the city.

And so, after ten long years of fighting, Menelaus recovered his beautiful Helen. Then he and the rest of the Greeks set sail for their native land.

Many of the Trojans were carried away into slavery by their Greek conquerors. An-drom´a-che, the beautiful wife of Hector, was given to the son of Achilles, who took her to his palace, as a captive.

Chapter IX

THE ADVENTURES OF ODYSSEUS

Part I

O dysseus (Roman name: Ulysses), king of the island of Ith´a-ca, had been very unwilling to go to the Trojan War because it had been prophesied that if he did go, he would not return home for twenty years. To avoid going to Troy, he pretended that he was mad. Yoking an ox and a horse together (something that was never done), he would plow the seashore, and sow the sand with salt.

Odysseus and Penelope

One of the chiefs suspected that all this was a trick. To test Odysseus he placed the king's infant son Te-le-ma´-chus in front of the plow. Odysseus at once turned the plow to one side and thus showed that he was not mad. He then had no excuse for staying at home and had to go to the war with the other chiefs.

All through the ten year long siege of Troy, he was of great value to the Greeks. After the death of Achilles, the splendid armor of that hero was given to Odysseus.

As soon as Troy had fallen, he set sail on his homeward voyage. If the winds had been fair he might have reached Ithaca in a month. But the story is that it took him ten years.

He had hardly begun his voyage when his fleet was caught in a storm and his ships

Ulytsses shows madness is pretense

were blown to the land of the lotus eaters. The lotus was a plant that made those who ate it forget their homes and friends forever. Two of Odysseus' sailors went on shore for only a few minutes, and having tasted this curious food became so anxious to stay with the lotus eaters that they had to be dragged back on board their ship.

After leaving the land of the lotus eaters, the fleet sailed to another shore. The sailors saw the mouth of a cavern and near it large flocks of sheep and goats. Odysseus, with twelve of his men, went to examine the cavern and see if anyone lived there. They carried with them a skin full of old wine to give to the king of the island if they should happen to meet him.

They entered the cave and saw pens for sheep and goats. They also found several baskets of cheese. It was plain that somebody lived in the place, so Odysseus decided to wait for the owner and buy some cheese from him. Meanwhile, he and the sailors helped themselves to what they wanted.

Just as the sun was setting, the bleating of sheep and goats was heard. Looking through the mouth of the cave, the Greeks saw the owner of the place coming toward them.

He was one of the race of giants called Cyclops, who had forged lightning and thunder for Zeus to use in the battles with Cronus. On his back the Cyclops carried a bundle of firewood. Before him went a flock of sheep and goats. The cave was a shelter for him and his flock.

When the giant had driven the sheep and goats inside, he followed them in and closed the entrance with a huge stone. Soon he set about milking the goats. As he milked, he muttered that thieves had stolen some of his cheeses. When the milking was over, he lit a fire on the floor of the cave and sat down to a supper of cheese and milk.

The fire lit up the corners of the cave where the Greeks had hidden themselves, and the Cyclops soon saw them.

"Who are you?" he growled. "And what business have you here?"

"Noble Sir," replied Odysseus, "we are Greeks from the island of Ithaca. With the rest of our nation we have fought against Troy for ten years. At last the city has fallen and now we are sailing homeward. A storm blew us to your island, and we landed to look for food. In the name of the blessed gods we ask you to give us something to eat, and let us go on our way."

"I care nothing for the gods!" roared the Cyclops. "But as for men — let me show you how much I like them!"

With that he seized two of the Greeks and ate them up, devouring even their bones. The other Greeks looked on in terror.

Soon after his supper the Cyclops went to sleep. Odysseus and his companions would have lost no time in killing him if it had not been for the great stone that blocked the door of the cave. All the Greeks together could not move it, and so they let the Cyclops live because in the morning he would roll the stone away.

Next morning, after devouring two more of the Greeks, he did move the stone. However, he put it right back as soon as he had driven out his flock. The Greeks were again shut up. In the evening, after the Cyclops had returned and had supped upon two more Greeks, Odysseus thought of his old wine and asked the giant to taste it. Taste it he did, and then quickly drained three cups.

"What is your name?" asked the Cyclops.

"Noman," answered Odysseus.

"Very well, Noman, you shall be the last that I will eat." And with that the giant lay down in a stupor.

Odysseus had sharpened the trunk of an olive tree that the Cyclops used for a walking cane, and he now held the sharp end in the fire until it glowed. Then with the help of four of his men, he rammed the red hot point into the giant's eye.

The monster roared so loudly that he wakened the other giants who lived in the caves nearby. They came running to ask who had hurt their companion.

"Noman!" screamed the Cyclops. "Noman has put out my eye!"

His friends, of course, understood him to mean that <u>no man</u> had hurt him. They thought that he had had a terrible nightmare from eating roast cheese, so they went back to their caves.

The Cyclops hurls stones at Odysseus

Odysseus now hit on a plan to get his friends and himself safely out of the cave. He bound the big long fleeced rams together, three abreast, and fastened a Greek under each middle ram so that every man was completely covered with fleece. He himself managed to cling to a ram that was the largest of the herd.

When the flock was passing out of the cave the Cyclops thought that perhaps the Greeks would try to ride out on the backs of the sheep and goats. He carefully felt the back of each animal as it went through the door. But he did not feel the Greeks, and they all got out safely.

Odysseus then untied his comrades, and they ran quickly to their ships, driving before them some of the sheep of the Cyclops. When the men and sheep were on board the vessels, Odysseus cried out, "Goodbye, Cyclops! What think you now of the gods? They sent me to punish you for your cruelty. Noman is not my name. I am Odysseus, Ithaca's king."

Part II

The next land they reached was an island on which Ae´o-lus, the god of the winds, had his home. Aeolus treated Odysseus very kindly. The west wind, which could carry the ships to Ithaca in nine days, the gods left free. He tied up all the other winds in a stout leather bag, which he gave to Odysseus. Odysseus then bade farewell to Aeolus.

For some time everything went well. One day, however, while Odysseus slept, his crew untied the wind bag, hoping to find money in it. As soon as the winds were set free, they blew the ships back to the islands of Aeolus, who drove them off. He thought that the gods were angry with them.

The fleet next reached an island where there were cannibals of great size and strength. They broke up all the ships except the one that Odysseus, himself, commanded, and they feasted on the sailors.

Odysseus made his escape on a single ship with those of his men that were left. He soon arrived at another island, on which at some distance from the shore, he saw a marble palace in the middle of the grove. He sent twenty-two men under the charge of his trusty captain, Eu-ry-lo´chus, to ask for food.

When Eurylochus reached the palace, he was met by a troop of lions, tigers and wolves, which capered about and fawned upon him and his men as so many playful puppies or kittens might do. This put Eurylochus on his guard. He made up his mind at once that the palace was the home of a wizard or a witch. At the palace gate he inquired "Who dwells here? We are strangers."

Circe and the crew of Odysseus

"Welcome!" replied a voice from within. "Welcome to the palace of the sun god's daughter. The best that is here shall be yours."

This was the voice of an enchantress called Cir´ce. It was her delight to turn men into brutes. The lions, tigers and wolves that had met Eurylochus were really men who had once sat at her table and drunk her enchanted wine.

Eurylochus refused to eat, but the men who went with him were a gluttonous set. They ate greedily and drank deeply. When the feast was at its height, Circe touched them with her wand and changed them into hogs.

Eurylochus returned to the ship and told what had happened. Odysseus then hastened to Circe's palace. On the way Hermes met him and walked with him for some distance. As they passed through a wood, the god plucked some flowers of a plant called moly and gave them to Odysseus.

"Smell them," said Hermes, "while Circe is talking to you and especially when you drink her enchanted wine."

When he reached the palace, the hero was welcomed as his comrades had been. Circe, herself, put a golden cup full of wine into his hand. Odysseus took the cup and drained it, taking care all the while to smell the moly that Hermes had given him in the wood.

When the cup was empty, the enchantress tapped the hero with her wand and said, "Now, turn into a pig and join your grunting companions."

Unchanged, however, Odysseus drew his sword and cried, "Wicked enchantress, you have no power over me. The gods have sent me here to punish you, and you shall die."

"I will undo what I have done if you will spare me," she cried.

So Odysseus followed her to the sty, where she touched the swine, one by one, with her magic wand. As each was touched, he was changed back to a man. Next the troop of lions, tigers, and wolves were touched, and they too were quickly changed back to men.

The other Greeks were then called from the ships, and Circe gave them a feast. After this Odysseus remained on her island for a whole year.

When at last he was going to sail, the enchantress gave him some good advice. On the homeward way, he and his men would have to pass close to the Isle of the Sirens, as the Argonauts had done long before them.

"To sail by the Sirens' Isle safely," said Circe, "let the men fill their ears with wax and lash you to the mast when the ship draws near to the Isle."

Odysseus and his men then left Circe's island. As they drew near to the Sirens' Isle, Odysseus made the sailors fill their ears with wax and lash him to the mast. As they rowed past the Sirens, sweet music came to him over the waters.

"Loose me!" Odysseus cried to the sailors. "Loose me. I must go nearer that music!" But the sailors rowed on. They could hear neither him nor the song of the Sirens.

"Slaves!" cried Odysseus, "Loose me!" But the sailors rowed on.

The music grew fainter and fainter. At last it died away, and the vessel was out of danger. Then the men took the wax from their ears and loosed the cords that bound their chief.

Part III

After passing the Sirens' Isle, Odysseus had to sail through a dangerous strait, now known as the Strait of Mes-si´na. In a rocky cave on one side of it dwelt a monster called Scyl´la that had six heads and six mouths. Each mouth could take in a whole man at once. Near the other side of the strait was Cha-ryb´dis, a whirlpool that sucked down all ships that came near it.

Odysseus saw that he could not escape both these dangers, and so to avoid Charybdis, he steered close to Scylla. He ordered his men to row as fast as they could past the monster's cave. The ship fairly spun through the water. But Scylla was also quick. Darting out all her heads at once, she seized six of the crew. While she was devouring them, the ship sped past her. Odysseus escaped with the rest of his men.

The hero now wished to continue his voyage without stopping, but his comrades were so tired that he agreed to land for the night on the coast of Sic´i-ly. So they pulled their ship up the sandy shore, and soon all were fast asleep.

In the morning a storm was howling about them. It would have been certain shipwreck to put to sea. The storm raged for a whole month, and even crafty Odysseus did not know what to do.

Worst of all, their provisions began to fail. So the sailors made up their minds to kill some of the famous fat cattle belonging to Apollo that were kept upon the island. Odysseus had been warned not to kill the animals and had ordered his men to leave them alone.

One day, however, when he was away, his crew killed some of the cattle. They lit a fire and were roasting several nice pieces of beef when suddenly, all started back in terror. The pieces of beef lowed as though they were living and the skins of the slaughtered oxen got up and began to switch their tails, toss their horns, and gallop up and down the shore.

The moment the tempest lulled, the men dragged their ship down the shore and pushed off as fast as they could.

They were not far out to sea when, suddenly, blackness covered the sky and a dreadful squall blew up. The ship went to pieces and all the men were drowned except Odysseus, who was washed up on the shore of a lonely island.

The island was the home of the sea-nymph Ca-lyp´so. She treated the shipwrecked hero most kindly and became so fond of him that she kept him with her seven years. She promised to make him immortal if he would stay with her always.

But Odysseus longed for home. So at last, Calypso led him to the other side of her island, and there he saw a forest of stately pine trees. With a keen bronze axe he soon felled twenty trunks. With these he built a raft, and bidding farewell to Calypso, set out on his homeward voyage.

Soon a storm arose. Heavy waves dashed over the raft and broke it into pieces. The hero clung to one log and drifted on it two days and two nights. The wind then lulled, and Odysseus, seeing land near, swam to the shore. Cold and tired, he gathered dry leaves, lay down upon them, and soon fell asleep. He slept all night and all the next morning.

At noon Nau-sic´-a-a, the daughter of the king of the island, went to the shore with her maidens. Their talking and laughing awakened Odysseus, and the princess, on hearing the tale of his shipwreck, took him home to her father's palace.

Here he was royally welcomed, and the very next day a ship was made ready. He was sent home to Ithaca.

When at dawn the ship reached Ithaca, Odysseus was so fast asleep that the crew carried him out of the vessel, wrapped in the rug on which he was sleeping. They laid him upon the sandy shore without waking him.

When he awoke he did not know where he was. But the goddess Athena appeared and told him that he was on his own island of Ithaca, and that Pe-nel´o-pe, his wife, loved him as much as ever. Then he climbed the rocky heights of the island and went to the cottage of his swineherd, who invited him in. Without telling the swineherd who he was, he stayed at the cottage that night.

Next morning there appeared at the swineherd's home Odysseus' son, Telemachus, who had just come back from a long search for his father. Odysseus made himself known to his son, and they talked over all that had happened while Odysseus had been so far away.

More than a hundred men from Ithaca and the neighboring isles had come to Odysseus' palace, hoping to marry Penelope. For months and years they had stayed at her palace, feasting and drinking at her expense, demanding that she should marry one of them. She told them that she could not wed until she had finished a shroud for her father-in-law, who was old and likely to die. She had spent years in making that shroud and even yet it was not finished — for every night she would undo the work she had woven during the day.

The suitors at last discovered the trick that Penelope was playing and refused to be put off any longer. They insisted that she must choose one of them for her husband. It was while they were doing this that Odysseus reached home.

He planned a way to punish the suitors. He first sent Telemachus to the palace alone to see his mother. Then, dressed as a beggar, Odysseus followed with the swineherd.

When he came to the palace gate in rags and tatters, no one knew who he was but his old dog, Argo. Argo recognized him at once and began licking his hand. The swineherd led the way into the banquet hall. A few paces behind him walked the ragged beggar, leaning upon a staff.

The swineherd kindly gave him a seat and invited him to eat and drink of the good cheer on the table. Hardly had Odysseus seated himself when jests and insults were heaped upon him by the suitors. It wrung the heart of Telemachus to see his father so badly used in his own palace, but he kept his temper and waited.

Not long after Odysseus' arrival, Penelope entered the banquet hall. She did not know that her husband had returned, but Athena had told her what to do. She stood beside one of the columns that upheld the roof of the hall and said, "Hear, all who are in this hall of Odysseus! You wish to take the place of my husband. I bring to you his bow. Whoever among you can bend and string it and with it shoot an arrow through twelve rings, him will I wed and him will I follow from this fair home."

Then the suitors, one by one, haughtily tried to string the bow. And, one by one, they utterly failed to bend it.

Odysseus then demanded that he, too, might try to bend the bow. Amid sneers and laughter, he was at length allowed to do so.

As easily as a skillful player stretches a chord from side to side of the harp, so without any effort, he strung the bow. Forthwith through each and all of the twelve rings, an arrow winged its way. It was followed by another which struck the chief man among the suitors dead. Telemachus and two faithful men, who had already locked the doors of the hall, now

Odysseus slays the suitors of Penelope

lent their aid to Odysseus. Arrows flew, swords flashed, and clubs were swung, until all the suitors who had tried to steal his wife and kingdom from Odysseus lay dead on the floor of the banquet hall.

Penelope's joy was great when she learned that the beggar was her husband. Odysseus' delight at finding that she still loved him made all his weary wanderings seem like a dream.

Chapter **X**

LYCURGUS

Part I

About eighty years after the Trojan War the descendants of Hercules invaded the Pel´o-pon-ne´sus, or the southern part of Greece, where Agamemnon and Menelaus had once lived. They captured Spar´ta and made it their capital. After that they called them-selves Spar´tans.

The Spartans made slaves of the people who were already living in the country and called them He´lots or captives. The conquerors divided the land among themselves and made the Helots work their farms.

After about three hundred years had passed, it seems that some of the Spartans had grown rich. Others had lost their land and slaves and become poor.

The Spartans who had lost their property were not willing to work like the slaves, and sometimes, when they had no bread for their children, bands of them would march through the streets of Sparta, break into the houses of the rich and take whatever they could lay their hands on.

During one of these riots, one of the two kings — for the Spartans always had two kings with equal power — went out of his palace to stop it. He tried to persuade the people to go quietly home, but they paid no attention to him and a butcher in the crowd stood up and stabbed him.

The murdered king left two sons. The elder became king, but soon died. The younger was named Ly-cur´gus. After his brother's death, everyone wished him to become king. But an infant child of the late king was the rightful heir, and Lycurgus refused to be anything more than regent.

For a while he ruled in the young king's name, but some of the people accused him of wishing to make himself king. So he gave up the regency and went traveling. He visited many lands and studied their forms of government. After being absent several years, he came back to Sparta. There he found that the rich were richer, and the poor were even more unhappy than they had been when he had gone away. Many felt that he was the only one who could help them.

He persuaded the people to let him make new laws for Sparta. The first change that he made was to give every Spartan a vote. There was a Senate of Thirty which might propose laws, but all the citizens were called together to pass or reject them.

Next he persuaded the rich people to divide their land fairly among all the citizens. So now no one had more than he needed, but everyone had a farm large enough to raise wheat and barley, olive oil and wine for his family for a year. No Spartan was permitted to work or to engage in any trade, but the slaves were divided. Every Spartan had slaves to work for him.

Besides the Spartans and the slaves, there was another class of men living on the lands of Sparta who were not slaves like the Helots, and yet not citizens like the Spartans. These men were farmers, traders, and mechanics. They had to pay taxes and fight when called upon, but neither they nor the Helots had anything to say about the government. There were about 10,000 pure Spartans and about 140,000 in the two lower classes, so you will see that the political power in Sparta was in the hands of very few men. Their government was what we would call an oligarchy, which means a government by the few.

Part II

Lycurgus did not wish the Spartans to become traders and grow rich, and it is said that he ordered their money to be made of iron. This iron money was worthless outside of Sparta, so the traders of other countries would not take it in payment for their goods and sold nothing to Spartans.

In those days soldiers fought chiefly with swords and spears, therefore, no matter how brave men were, they had to have physical strength to win a victory. Lycurgus made laws that the men and boys of Sparta should be trained in running, boxing, wrestling, throwing quoits, hurling javelins, and shooting with bows and arrows. The girls had nearly the same training.

The feeble and deformed were thought by Lycurgus to be useless. Infants were therefore examined after birth and those that were weak or deformed were killed. A strong, well-formed infant was handed back to its parents with the order, "Bring up this child for Sparta."

Boys remained at home until they were seven years old. Then they were taken in charge by the State to be trained. The clothing given them was scanty. They went about with their heads and feet bare, and slept on hard beds, or even on floors, with rushes instead of a mattress.

Young Spartans learing from drunken Helots

To teach the boys temperance, Helots were sometimes purposely made drunk. Thus the boys saw how foolish men become when they drink too much.

One lesson that every Spartan boy had to learn was to endure pain without flinching. Another was that in battle a man might die, but must not surrender. When the young Spartan was leaving for the field of battle his mother would hand him his shield and say, "Come back with this, or upon this."

Lycurgus was opposed to all expensive ways of living. He thought that luxury was a waste of money and made men weak and effeminate. He made a law that the men should not take their meals at home but in a public dining hall; and there only the simplest kind of food was set before them — bread, cheese, olive oil, and a kind of black broth that was probably made of black beans. Figs and grapes were served for dessert. It is said that some rich people were very angry because they had to eat at the public tables and that one young man threw stones at Lycurgus.

A great change came over the Spartans after they had adopted the new laws and ways of living. Instead of being a nation of idlers they became so strong and brave that when there was talk of building a wall around the city, Lycurgus said, "Sparta's citizens are her walls."

When Lycurgus saw what improvement had been made, he told the people that he was going on a long journey. He made them promise that they would not change his laws until he returned.

He never returned. When the Spartans felt sure that he was dead they built a temple in his honor and worshiped him as a god. He left Sparta about 825 B.C. and his laws were not changed for several hundred years. They made Sparta the most powerful military state in Greece.

Chapter XI

DRACO AND SOLON

Part I

One of the first Athenians whose acts belong to history is Dra´co, who lived about 600 years before Christ.

At that time the working people of Athens were very unhappy. One reason for this was that the laws were not written, and the judges were very unfair. They almost always decided in favor of their rich friends. At last, everybody in Athens agreed that the laws ought to be written out, and Draco was asked to write them.

Some old laws were so severe that often people had been put to death for very slight offenses. Draco changed these severe laws and made new ones a great deal more merciful, and this made the people very fond of him. A story is told about his death which shows that other people besides the Athenians thought a great deal of him. He went to a theater not far from Athens. When the audience in the theater saw him, they threw to him their cloaks and capes as an honor to him. Unfortunately, such a pile of cloaks fell on him that he was smothered to death.

Even after the laws had been written down, the people were not entirely happy. Although Draco did change some of the harsher laws, he had not changed some of the laws that bore very hard upon the poor. These were the laws concerning debts. If a man borrowed money and could not pay it back at the right time, the man who had lent the money had the right to take the borrower's house and farm. He might even sell the debtor, his wife, and his children as slaves. On most of the farms near Athens, stone pillars were set up, each of which told that the land on which it stood was mortgaged, or pledged, for a debt. Many of the farmers and their families had been sold as slaves. In time it came to be said that Draco's laws were written in blood.

Part II

Happily, a very wise and good man called So´lon was then living in Athens. The Athenians turned to him, asking him to make a new set of laws.

Rich and poor were surprised when they read Solon's new laws. The poor who had lost their farms and houses were to have everything given back to them. Solon thought that they had paid so much interest for so many years that the original debts had been more than paid for and should be forgiven. All who had been sold as slaves were to have their freedom, and no one was ever again to be sold into slavery in order to repay a debt. Those debtors who had not lost everything were to be forgiven about a quarter of the amount they owed.

Solon defending his laws

All of this Solon called a "shaking off of burdens," and thousands of people felt that heavy burdens had indeed been taken from their shoulders.

Solon did another good thing for the people. He gave every citizen a vote in the Assembly of the people. This Assembly was much like a New England town meeting. There was also a Senate of Four Hundred, which proposed laws, but it was the people themselves who either passed or rejected them. So it was that the people of Athens really made their own laws.

In addition to this, every nine years the Assembly was to choose nine ar´chons, as the rulers of Athens were to be called. The chief archon was like the mayor of one of our cities and the others like the aldermen. Under Solon's new laws, Athens soon came to stand for government by all the people, just as Sparta stood for government by only a few of the people.

Part III

When Solon saw that his laws were making the Athenians contented and prosperous, he made them promise not to change them for ten years. He then went on a long journey.

One of the countries which he visited was Lyd´i-a in Asia Minor. Croe´sus, the king of Lydia, was called the richest man in the world. He was so famous for his wealth that even now you often hear people say that a man is "as rich as Croesus."

Croesus was very proud of being so rich and wished Solon to flatter him. He asked Solon, "Who is the happiest man you have ever known?" He expected the Athenian of course to say, "Yourself, your Majesty."

Solon however replied, "An Athenian peasant who never suffered want, who had a good wife and children, and who died on the battlefield for his country."

"Who is the next happiest?" asked Croesus.

"The next two happiest persons whom I have known," said Solon, "were the sons of a certain priestess of Hera. It was her duty to offer a sacrifice in the temple. When the time came for her to go, the oxen to draw the cart could not be found. So her sons yoked themselves to the ox cart and drew her all the way to the temple. She was so much pleased at this that she prayed to Juno to grant her sons the greatest blessing that they could have.

The mother's prayer was answered, for the sons lay down to sleep in the temple and never waked. They had done their parts well in the world, and they left it without pain or sorrow, beloved and admired by all who knew them."

"But," cried Croesus, "do you not think a rich and powerful king like me is happy?"

"Ah, Croesus," said Solon, "I call no man happy until he is dead. You are rich. You are king of thousands of people. You live a life of luxury. But none of these things proves you happy. When I hear whether or not your life has ended nobly, then I shall know whether or not you were really happy."

Years afterward when Croesus had lost his kingdom and his wealth, he saw how wise this speech of Solon was.

After ten years of travel, Solon returned to Athens where he lived in honor until his death.

Chapter XII

PISISTRATUS THE TYRANT

Part I

When Solon came back from his travels, he found that a young kinsman of his, named Pi-sis´tra-tus, was trying to make himself master of Athens. Pisistratus was rich and gave away a great deal of money, and in every possible way showed himself friendly to the people. His large and beautiful garden was thrown open to them as if it were a park. Men and women of the working classes were allowed to sit under his shade trees, and their children played among his flowers. When the poor were ill, he had nice things cooked for them in his own kitchen. Often, in the heat of summer, he sent to the sick a present of snow, which was a rare luxury. If a poor man died, Pisistratus often paid the expense of burying him. Poor people in Athens were very much pleased by this, because they believed that if a person were not properly buried, his soul would have to wander a hundred years up and down the bank of the river Styx.

One day, after the kindness of Pisistratus had made him the idol of the Athenians, he drove his chariot rapidly into the market place. A crowd immediately gathered about him, for they saw that something was the matter. In a state of great excitement he showed some wounds — which he had really made upon himself, but which he pretended he had received while he was driving along the high road.

"Men of Athens!" he cried, "I got these wounds because I spoke for the people!" All saw the blood on his face and, of course, believed what he said. They were very angry, and one of them proposed in the public Assembly that in the future, fifteen men, armed with clubs, should be paid by the state to guard Pisistratus.

Solon begged the people to vote against this. But they had made up their minds. Solon could not dissuade them. The guard was ordered, and Pisistratus took good care that there should be in it a great many more than fifty men. Very soon he had a company of soldiers who were ready to do whatever he ordered. So, just as Solon had feared, Pisistratus seized the A-crop´o-lis, a high, rocky hill which was the citadel of Athens, and made himself master of the city.

After a while the people grew tired of Pisistratus, and he had to leave Athens. However, he came back and regained his power by playing a trick on the people. A very tall and beautiful girl, in full armor, rode into the city standing at his side in a chariot. Athena, herself, was said to be bringing Pisistratus back. When the chariot came into view, the people shouted with joy and welcomed their old friend.

Soon, he was banished a second time. Again, he recovered his power, and from that day to the time of his death, he held full sway over the city.

Part II

All the states of Greece had, in time, become republics, except Sparta. When anyone took the power of a king in any of these states, he was called a tyrant. Thus, Pisistratus was called the Tyrant of Athens. Yet, he was by no means so harsh a ruler as the word "tyrant" might lead us to think. He was strict. When he got control of Athens it was full of lazy people who lounged all day about the market place. Pisistratus put all such people to work upon the roads or public buildings.

There were no public schools or libraries in Athens, but Pisistratus did his best to give the people a chance to read and to educate themselves. Books in his days were not printed, but written by hand, and they were so expensive that few people could buy them. Pisistratus had a large collection of books, and he invited all persons, rich or poor, to go to his library and read.

He did another thing for which the Greeks were grateful. For more than two hundred years before his time, the poems of Ho´mer had been recited all over Greece. Traveling minstrels sang them before guests in banquet halls, or before public gatherings. Everyone loved these poems, and many people knew parts of them by heart. Pisistratus employed learned men to help him write them and put them in proper order. The verses about the Trojan War were arranged to make up the poem called the Il´i-ad, and those about the wanderings of Odysseus to make up the poem called the Od´ys-sey.

Many feel that Athens never had a wiser or better ruler than Pisistratus. He died in the year 527 B.C.

Chapter XIII

MILTIADES
THE HERO OF MARATHON

Part I

After Pisistratus died, his two sons, Hip´pi-as and Hip-par´chus, ruled over Athens. They governed well until Hipparchus was killed by his enemies. Then Hippias became so cruel that the Athenians banded together and drove him out of the city.

Some time after being driven from Athens, Hippias went to Asia and begged Da-ri´us, king of Persia, to help him regain his power. At that time, Persia was the greatest country in the world. Darius, her sovereign, was called the "Great King," or simply "the King," as if there were no other king on the face of the earth. He intended that there should be no other kings. He made up his mind not only to help Hippias, but also to make himself the master of Greece. Persian heralds were therefore sent to every state of Greece to demand from each a tribute of earth and water. If the Greeks had yielded to this demand, it would have been the same as saying that all the land and water of Greece belonged to Persia. Some of the states submitted to Darius. Others proudly refused. The Athenians threw the heralds into a ditch into which the bodies of criminals were thrown. The Spartans threw them into a well and told them, "There you will find both earth and water for your master."

As soon as Darius heard of this he declared war. Soon his fleet, carrying one hundred and fifty thousand men, set sail for Greece. The Persians landed on the Grecian coast and went into camp on the plain of Mar´a-thon, twenty-two miles from Athens.

Meantime the Athenians had not been idle. They had collected an army of ten thousand men. The entire army was under two generals, each of whom in turn was commander for a day. The little city of Pla-tae´a, unasked, had sent a thousand volunteers.

The ablest of the Greek generals was Mil-ti´a-des. He determined to attack the enemy at once, and when his day of command came, on the 12th of August, 490 B.C., he drew up the Greek army in line of battle and moved across the plain. Then he charged upon the Persian army, broke their line, and drove them back to their ships in confusion.

News of the victory was carried to Athens by a soldier, who, though wounded, ran the twenty-two miles from the field of battle to the city. Reaching the market place, he rushed into the crowd of citizens assembled there, and crying "Rejoice! Rejoice! We are victors!" fell dead.

The news of the victory delighted all loyal Athenians, but was very unwelcome to some traitors who had been hoping to hear of a Persian victory. These traitors had gone to a mountain near Athens, and with a polished shield had flashed a signal to the Persian fleet telling them to sail to Athens and capture the city before Miltiades could return from Marathon.

Fortunately, the signal was seen in the camp of the Greeks. Miltiades guessed what it meant and marched back to Athens immediately. When the Persians approached in their ships, they realized that they would have to meet the army of Miltiades again if they landed. Because they had no desire to do this, they sailed away across the Aegean Sea to the Great King's own dominions.

The battle of Marathon showed that the Greeks were equal to any soldiers in the world. They had routed an army of Persians fifteen times as large as their own, and had lost only one hundred and ninety-two men.

The Greeks believed that this splendid victory was won through the aid of their gods and of their god-like hero, Theseus, who was said to have fought in the thick of the battle and made terrible havoc among the Persians.

Part II

Miltiades won great fame in Athens. Honors were showered upon him and whatever he asked was granted. Thinking that it would add still more to his own glory, and that of Athens, he asked the city of Athens to place a fleet of seventy ships at his command.

His request was granted, and he set sail for the island of Pa´ros. The people of Paros had helped the Persians in the recent war, and Miltiades wished to punish them. He also hoped to avenge himself upon a personal enemy. The expedition was a complete failure. The town of Paros was not captured, and Miltiades was obliged to give up the siege and return to Athens.

Moreover, at Paros, Miltiades' thigh had been badly hurt as he was leaping over a fence. Miltiades came home injured as well as unsuccessful. Upon his return he was accused of having deceived the people and wasted the public money.

When his trial took place, he was brought before his judges upon a couch, being too weak to stand or sit. The decision of the court was against him, and he was sentenced to a heavy fine. He did not have enough money to pay the fine. Not long afterwards, he died of the injury he had received at Paros.

After the death of Miltiades, the Athenians were sorry that they had been so harsh in their treatment of him. Remembering only his heroism at Marathon, they buried him with the highest honors on the plain where his great victory was won.

Chapter XIV

LEONIDAS AT THERMOPYLAE

Leonidas was a son of one of the kings of Sparta. As a boy he had been trained in the gymnasium and excelled in all manly sports. As a man he fought in the Spartan army. After the death of his father and his half-brother, he became king. Eleven years later he led the Greek army against the Persians, who were threatening Greece for a second time. The second invasion of the Persians came about in this way.

The defeat at Marathon had made Darius all the more determined to conquer the Greeks. But four years after that defeat, as he was making preparations for another attack, Darius died. His son, Xerx´es, came to the throne.

After a while Xerxes decided to carry out his fathers plans to launch another attack on Greece. He spent four years collecting men and horses and ships. His army and fleet were the largest that the world had ever heard of.

The land forces met at Sar´dis, a city in Asia Minor, and marched to the shore of the Hellespont, which you have already learned, is the narrow strait between Europe and Asia. Xerxes ordered his engineers to make two bridges of boats across the strait for the passage of the army. This was done, but the bridges were not strong enough, and a storm destroyed them. The loss of his bridges made the king very angry. It is said that he ordered his soldiers to scourge the waters with three hundred lashes and then throw a set of chains into it to teach the water that he was its master.

Two new bridges, stronger than the first, were built and Xerxes then marched his army over them to the European shore of the Hellespont. Here his fleet of twelve hundred ships and three thousand smaller vessels had already arrived. On a hill overlooking the strait, a throne of marble was built. Upon it Xerxes sat and reviewed his land forces drawn up along the shore, and his ships sailing in the strait. It took the army seven days and seven nights to cross the bridges.

After crossing, the land force made its way southward until it reached a high and almost impassable mountain range. Between this range and the sea was a point so narrow that only a single wagon had room enough to pass. The Greeks called this narrow part of the road Ther-mop´y-lae, which means "Gates of the Hot Springs," because of the hot sulphur springs nearby.

The Persians intended to march through the Pass of Thermopylae, but they were stopped by a Greek force commanded by Le-on´i-das, king of Sparta. His band of men numbered only about four thousand men. Three hundred of these men were from Sparta, the rest came from several different states.

The Greeks took their stand at the narrowest part of the Pass. Against them, Xerxes sent one division of his army after another. All were defeated and driven back. For two days the fighting went on with great loss to the Persians. The Greeks, however, lost hardly a man.

At last, when it seemed that the Persians were lost, a Greek traitor showed a band of Persians a path that led over the mountain. This pass was poorly defended by Greeks from one of the northern states. It was easily taken by the Persians who then marched around behind Leonidas.

Leonidas learned of their approach in time to escape. Some of his army did retreat; but he, with three hundred Spartans and seven hundred men from a little town of Thes´pi-ae, refused to do so. Greece had trusted the Pass to them to hold, and they preferred to die rather than leave their post. When someone said that the arrows of the Persians would come in such showers as to conceal the sun, one of the Spartans replied, "So much the better; we shall fight in the shade."

Leonidas was now penned in between two divisions of the Persian army, one at each end of the Pass. Instead of waiting to be attacked, he led his men forward against the Persians. The Greeks fought desperately, but they had no chance against such vast numbers. All but one man was slain.

Afterwards, a monument was raised to their memory. It bore the simple inscription, "Stranger, tell the Spartans that we lie here in obedience to their commands."

After the battle, Xerxes marched to Athens. He found it almost deserted. All the Athenians had fled, except for a little band who held the Acropolis. They hurled rocks upon the attacking Persians, and for a long time they were able to resist them. At length, however, the Persians found a place where no guard had been stationed because the rocky wall was so steep that the Athenians thought it would be impossible to climb. The Persians rushed up the wall and charged in upon the brave defenders.

The capture of the Acropolis

The struggle was soon over. Some of the Athenians hurled themselves headlong down the rock slopes. The rest were put to death, and the city fell into the hands of the Persians. The conquering army plundered and burned the city. Even the sacred olive tree, believed to have sprung up at Athena's touch, was burned to the ground.

Chapter XV

THEMISTOCLES

Part I

At this time the leading man of Athens was a great statesman and soldier named The-mis´to-cles. Some years before, when the news had come that Xerxes was collecting an army and intended to invade Greece, the Athenians sent messengers to Delphi to ask the oracle what they should do. Delphi was upon the side of Mount Parnassus, and there stood a temple of Apollo. It was built over the cleft in the rock which, you remember, Deucalion found long ago as he and Pyrrha were coming down the mountain after the flood.

In the inner chamber of the temple, just over the cleft, was a three-legged stool called a tripod. When a person wished to consult the oracle, the Priestess, who was called the Pyth´i-a, took her seat on the tripod. In a few minutes her eyes would close and she would begin to talk. The words which she spoke were noted, and the Greeks believed that they were really the words of the god Apollo.

Her answer to the messengers from Athens was, "When everything else in the land of Ce´crops should be taken, Zeus grants to Athens that the wooden wall alone shall remain undestroyed, and it shall defend you and your children. Stand not to await the attack of horses and foot from Asia, but retire. You shall live to fight another day. And thou, O divine Sa-la´mis, shalt destroy the children of women!"

What do you think this strange answer meant? The Athenians were greatly puzzled by it.

The Pythia on the tripod

Themistocles decided that the "wooden wall" meant ships of war, and that the gods would save the people if they would leave their city and trust in their fleet when the enemy approached. He advised the Athenians to build more ships of war. The people at last came to believe him. Rich Athenians gave him money, and the people voted that the silver which was dug every year from the silver mines owned by the city should be used to pay for building ships of war. And thus by the time Xerxes began his march, Athens had a fleet of two hundred ships of war. These vessels were gigantic rowboats, each having as many as a hundred and fifty oars. Each also had a mast with a single big sail, which was hoisted to help the rowers.

The capture of Thermopylae had given the Persians an open road to Athens, and so the women and children of the city and the men who were too old to fight had been sent away in merchant ships to places of safety. A few men stayed in Athens and defended the citadel, as you learned in the last chapter. The rest went out in the war ships with Themistocles to fight behind the "wooden wall."

Part II

Themistocles and the commanders of the fleets of the other Greek states took their vessels into the narrow strait of Salamis, which lay between the island of Salamis and the shore of Attica. Here the Persians followed them. Themistocles now wished the Greeks to give battle to the Persians, but the Spartan commander and the other Greek leaders were unwilling to risk a battle in the narrow strait. They proposed to retreat. Themistocles was determined, however, that a battle should be fought in the strait. He sent word secretly to Xerxes that the Greek ships were going to try to get away and advised him to head them off.

Xerxes watching the battle of Salamis

The great naval battle at Salamis

Xerxes was delighted to get this message. During the night he sent a part of his fleet up the shore of Attica to the other end of the strait, so as to hem the Greek fleet in between two lines of Persian ships. Next morning the Greek leaders all saw that there was nothing to do but fight, and at once their ships were drawn up in the line of battle.

Xerxes' throne had been placed on a high cliff on the shore of Attica, so that he might look down upon the battle. When the sun rose he took his seat upon the throne. He was clothed in his royal robes and surrounded by the princes of his court. Below him were a thousand Persian war vessels, while close to the shore of the island lay three hundred and seventy-eight Greek vessels. It seemed an easy victory for the Persians. The Greeks rowed forward from the shore of Salamis, shouting the cry, "We fight for all." The Persians replied with their war cry, and the battle began. For a time the Persians had the advantage. But their ships were in the way of one another; those in the front could not go back, those in the rear could not come forward. The confusion became terrible. Ship after ship of the Persians sank, some of them rammed by the Greeks, others run down by their own allies. In all, two hundred Persian vessels were destroyed and a great number were captured. The Greeks lost only forty ships.

When Xerxes saw his thousand vessels sunk or captured or rowing away in flight, he determined to go back to Persia.

He at once returned to northern Greece, where he left 300,000 men in the command of his brother-in-law, Mar-don´ius. With the rest of his army he marched on to the Hellespont.

Here he found that storms had destroyed his bridges, so that what was left of his army was carried across to the shore of Asia Minor in ships.

Part III

Everybody in Greece now admitted that Themistocles had been right in his explanation of the oracle. The "wooden wall" had saved the people. And "Salamis," as the oracle had said, "destroyed the sons of women" — chiefly the sons of Persian, not Greek women.

The battle of Salamis brought fresh glory to Themistocles. After some years, however, he became unpopular and was banished from Athens. He stayed at Argos. Then the Spartans, who were his enemies, accused him of treason against Greece. Fearing that he could not get a fair trial at Athens, he fled to Persia.

The Persian king gave him three cities with which to support himself, and in one of these he lived until his death in 453 B.C.

Chapter XVI

ARISTIDES THE JUST

Part I

Ar-is-ti′des was the rival of Themistocles. Themistocles was wise and brave, but selfish and fond of money. Aristides, too, was wise and brave, but he was also so honorable in his dealings that the Athenians called him "The Just."

On one occasion he was acting as judge between two men. One of them had spoken unfairly of Aristides and the other came secretly to Aristides to tell him of it. "My friend," said Aristides, "tell me the wrong the man has done to you, not what he had done to me. It is not my cause that I am to decide, but yours."

Aristides opposed many plans that Themistocles wished to carry out, and so at length, Themistocles determined to have Aristides banished.

There was at Athens a curious way of getting rid of a citizen. Every year this question was put before the people, "Does the safety of the state require that any citizen be banished?" If it was decided that this was necessary the people were called upon to vote. No person's name was mentioned, but every citizen wrote on a small earthenware tablet the name of any man whom he thought dangerous to the state. The tablets were collected and counted. If the name of any one man was written on as many as 6,000 tablets, he had to leave the city for ten years. Banishing people in this way was called "ostracism." We often use the word today. It comes from a Greek word meaning an earthenware tablet.

Themistocles and his friends persuaded many of the Athenians that Aristides was a dangerous citizen. So when a public meeting was being held, the people were asked if

Aristides and the countryman

they thought any citizen ought to be banished. No one mentioned Aristides' name, but Themistocles' friends said, "Let a vote be taken." While the vote was being cast, a countryman who could not write his own name came up to Aristides and said, "Friend, will you write the name of Aristides for me on this tablet?"

"Has Aristides ever wronged you?" asked Aristides gently.

"No," said the other, "I have never seen him, but I am tired of hearing him called *the Just.*"

Aristides said no more, but wrote his own name on the tablet.

There were enough votes against Aristides to banish him. As he was leaving Athens, he prayed to the gods asking that the time might never come when his fellow citizens should have cause to be sorry for what they had done.

That time came, however. Three years later when Athens was threatened by the Persians, the citizens, at the request of Themistocles, himself, recalled Aristides. He sailed from his place of exile to the bay of Salamis and went on board the ship of Themistocles only a few hours before the famous battle. Themistocles at once gave him command of one of the Athenian ships, and he did good service in battle.

Part II

In the spring following the battle of Salamis, Mardonius, the Persian commander in Thes´sa-ly, tried to bribe the Athenians to become allies of the great king. They refused his offers with scorn. He then marched to Athens and people abandoned the city, so that it fell into his hands.

The Greeks, however, collected an army of one hundred and ten thousand men. Pau-sa´ni-as, a nephew of Leonidas, the hero of Thermopylae, was made commander-in-chief; but Aristides commanded the Athenian troops. Mardonius now retreated from Athens, destroying and burning as he went. The Greeks followed and overtook him near the city of Pla-tae´a, and there they defeated him in one of the "decisive battles of the world." Mardonius himself was killed.

It took ten days to divide the spoil and bury the dead. A tenth of the spoil was sent to Delphi and dedicated to Apollo, because of the promise by his oracle that the "wooden wall would save the city" had led to the great victory of Salamis. A temple was erected to Athena, and thank offerings were made to other gods. "Liberty games" were established, to be held on the battlefield once in four years. It was also decreed that every year the tombs of those who had fallen in battle were to be decorated with flowers. The land upon which Plataea stood was declared sacred, and the inhabitants of the city were to be always free from attack by the other Greeks.

On the afternoon of the very day on which the battle of Plataea was won, the Greek fleet gained a great victory over the Persians at Myc´a-le, on the coast of Asia Minor. After their defeats at Marathon, at Plataea, and at Mycale, the Persians never again attempted to conquer Greece.

Part III

As soon as the victory at Plataea had freed Greece from the ravaging Persian army, the Athenians flocked back to their ruined city and began to rebuild it. Aristides and Themistocles carried on this work hand in hand.

It was found that the sacred olive tree on the Acropolis, though burned to the ground, was not killed. From its root a stout young shoot had sprung. This was taken by the citizens as a good omen, and the rebuilding of the city went on rapidly. The great seaport called the Pi-rae´us was fortified, and a wall was built around the city.

These and other public works required a great outlay of money, and it was needful to put someone whom all the citizens trusted in charge of the funds raised. Aristides was chosen, and enormous sums of money were placed in his hands. He used his office solely for the good of the people and never became rich.

When he died in about 468 B.C., the whole nation mourned, and he was buried at public expense.

skip

Chapter XVII

CIMON

Part I

You remember that when Xerxes was preparing to invade Greece, Themistocles tried to get the Athenians to build ships and quit their city, and trust in the "wooden wall" of a fleet.

One day, while the people were still in doubt about what they should do, a tall and handsome young man, with a bridle in his hand, was seen hurrying through the streets of Athens toward the Acropolis. He entered the temple of Athena, hung up his bridle as an offering to the goddess, and took a shield down from the wall. He prayed to the goddess and then carried the shield through the streets of Athens to the Piraeus.

The young man was named Ci´mon. He was the son of the famous Miltiades and belonged to a class of Athenians called knights. The knights fought on horseback. For him to hang up his bridle in the temple was just like saying that Athens now had no need of horsemen, but of seamen, just as Themistocles was urging.

People were fond of young Cimon because of his pleasant ways. When they saw that he thought well of Themistocles' advice, a great many who had not liked it changed their minds.

Cimon himself sailed in the Athenian fleet and fought bravely in the battle of Salamis. He distinguished himself so much that not long after the Persians had been driven from

81

Greece he was elected admiral of the fleet.

At that time there were a number of pirates living on the island of Scyros, in the Aegean Sea. They captured the merchant vessels that carried on the trade of the Mediterranean. Cimon took possession of their island and made the Aegean Sea safe for traders.

The island was the one on which Thetis was said to have tried to hide Achilles when the Trojan War began. Somewhere upon it, Theseus, the great hero of Athens, had been buried. Cimon made a search for the burial place and found it. He took the bones out of the tomb and carried them to Athens.

When he arrived at Athens and told that he had brought the bones of Theseus, the whole city was filled with rejoicing. Games were held, and theatrical exhibitions were given. The great poets Aes´chy-lus and Soph´o-cles wrote plays for the occasion.

Cimon took so much booty from the pirates that after a while he became very wealthy. He was also very generous. His fine gardens were open to the public and people were allowed to gather fruit in his orchard. The Athenians said, "He got riches so he could use them, and then used them so that he got honor." His fellow citizens almost worshipped him.

Part II

After some years of fighting, the allies of Athens grew tired of warfare. So Cimon agreed to let them furnish ships and money, and he hired seamen and marines from among the Athenians. Though the fleet was in name the fleet of Greece, it was really Athenian. He drilled his men well in naval warfare and took them on one expedition after another. Thus they became the finest sea soldiers in Greece.

At one time Cimon learned that there was a Persian fleet off the coast of Asia Minor. Immediately, two hundred ships were made ready, and he sailed to attack the Persians. The Persian fleet was about twice the size of Cimon's fleet, but the Greeks destroyed a great number of Persian vessels and captured two hundred of their ships.

Cimon then disembarked his men and fought a Persian army on land. He completely defeated it and so gained two victories in one day. Immediately after this, he was told that another Persian fleet was not far off. At once he sailed to the spot and destroyed or captured all the ships and the men upon them.

The Persian king was not glad to make peace. He agreed that no army of his should ever go nearer to the Aegean Sea than a day's journey on horseback — about fifty miles — and that none of his warships would ever sail near Greece.

The spoil taken on Cimon's great expedition was immense. It sold for so much that the Athenians took part of the money to pay for building the foundations of the great walls called the "Long Walls." These walls were to connect Athens with her ports and serve as fortifications. Cimon paid for part of this work out of his own share of the spoils.

It seems strange that the Athenians should ever have turned against Cimon after all his victories. Yet they did.

A terrible earthquake happened in Sparta. The whole city was ruined and only five houses stood unharmed after the shock. One large building fell upon some of the young men and boys who were drilling and killed them.

While everything was in confusion and everybody was filled with alarm, the Helots flocked together from the fields, intending to massacre their masters. Fortunately, one of the kings heard in time that the Helots were arming themselves. He at once ordered an alarm to be given by sounding trumpets. The Spartans seized their shields and spears and gathered together. When the Helots reached the city and saw the citizens ready to resist them, they went back into the country.

But because they had a large and powerful army, they were able to persuade some neighbors of the Spartans to join them. Then they seized a strong fortress near Sparta.

The Spartans were now in a dreadful plight. Their homes were in ruins, their slaves in revolt, and their neighbors were aiding the slaves.

In their distress they sent to the Athenians for aid. The great comic poet Ar´is-toph´a-nes said, "There was a wonderful difference between the scarlet robe and white cheeks of the Spartan who came to ask us for troops."

Some of the Athenians advised that no troops should be sent. They thought it would be a good thing for Athens if Sparta lost her power. The two cities were rivals. But Cimon persuaded his countrymen to send a large force. He said, "Athens and Sparta are the two legs of Greece. Do not suffer Greece to be maimed and Athens to lose her companion."

So Athenian soldiers went in command of Cimon and fought for the Spartans. But the Helots and their allies were too strong. The fortress was not taken. Then the Spartans suspected that the Athenians had not done their best. They said that they wanted no more help from Athens.

This made the people of Athens very angry. They were enraged not only with the Spartans but with Cimon as well. They declared that any friend of Sparta was an enemy of Athens, and so they banished Cimon.

Part III

After the Spartans had conquered their slaves, they sent an army to attack Athens. A battle was fought not far from the city and the Spartans gained the victory.

Then someone was needed in Athens who could either beat the Spartans or make friends with them. Cimon was therefore recalled from banishment. Not long after his return he made a truce with the Spartans that lasted for several years.

Cimon thought that the best way to keep peace in Greece was to fight with the Persians. So he fitted out a fleet and set sail from Athens to attack parts of the "Great King's" dominions.

He really hoped to overthrow the whole Persian empire. Before making any attack, he sent friends to the oracle of Zeus. (The god refused to answer the question that they put and gave as a reason,) "Because Cimon is already with me." The messengers wondered what this could mean, but when they reached the Greek fleet, they found that Cimon was dead.

Some say he died of sickness, others of a wound he had received while besieging a city.

Before he died he ordered his officers to conceal his death from the soldiers and to carry his body to Athens. This they did.

Chapter XVIII

PERICLES

Part I

Cimon had a rival named Per´i-cles who was the most able leader Athens ever had. He had the power of a tyrant, but he used it for the welfare of the people.

He had many excellent laws passed. One law required a man accused of any crime to be tried by a certain number of his fellow citizens. This was like our trial by jury, and it gave an Athenian the same rights in a trial that an American citizen has today. Another good law proposed by Pericles said that any citizen who fought in the army or the navy of Athens should be paid for doing so. Still another of his laws said that a poor man who wished to go to the theater might get the money from the city treasurer to pay for his seat.

You will remember that Themistocles and Aristides began to rebuild and beautify Athens after it had been burned by the Persians. This work was afterwards carried on by Pericles. It was said that he found Athens a city of brick and left it a city of marble.

Under his order the white marble Par´the-non, the temple of Athena, was erected on the Acropolis. It was one of the most beautiful buildings in the world.

In front of it stood a bronze statue of Athena, so large that it could be seen far out at sea. Within the temple was another splendid statue of the goddess, nearly thirty feet high, which was made of ivory and gold.

Pericles made Athens strong as well as beautiful. He finished the "Long Walls" which Cimon had begun. These walls were built from the city to her ports, which were about four miles away. Between two of the walls was a roadway, by which provisions could be safely carried from the harbor to the city in time of war.

Sparta was not pleased to hear of the fortifications of her rival. Athens might make herself beautiful if she chose, but she must not make herself strong. The Spartans watched for an opportunity to quarrel with the Athenians, and the opportunity soon came. The people of Cor-cy´ra, an island now called Cor´fu, lying off the west coast of Greece, went to war with the people of Corinth. Athens helped the Cor´cy-re-ans; Sparta, the Corinthians.

This was the beginning of a contest between Sparta and Athens which desolated Greece for twenty-seven years (431 B.C. to 404 B.C.). It is called the Peloponnesian War, because most of the states in the Pel-o-pon-ne´sus took part in it and were allies of Sparta. Athens also had her allies.

Athens was well prepared for war. She had a large sum of money in her treasury, a good fleet, and about thirty thousand soldiers whom she could put into the field.

The Spartans brought a force of sixty thousand men into Attica to attack Athens. Pericles then urged the country people to leave their farms and homes and come into the city. They took his advice, and every vacant spot in Athens was filled with huts and tents. Pericles thought that Athens, protected by the "Long Walls," could withstand any siege.

In this he was right, for the Spartans made no headway; but very soon the Athenians were attacked by a foe far more terrible than the Spartans. This was the plague. So many people were huddled together in the city that it was impossible to keep it clean and healthy. People began to sicken and die by dozens, then by hundreds. The Spartans, fearing that the plague might attack them, retreated across the Isthmus of Corinth into Peloponnesus.

While Athens was in this desperate condition, Pericles acted most nobly. The plague carried off his eldest son, his sister, and many of his closest friends. Yet he went among the people, calming and cheering them, and attending faithfully to the affairs of the government. It was only when he laid the funeral wreath upon the lifeless body of his favorite son that he broke down and sobbed and shed a flood of tears.

While the Spartan army was threatening Athens, and when the plague came, many of the Athenians blamed Pericles. But when he was in sorrow all Athens showed him the greatest respect and affection.

Not long after the death of his son, he himself was stricken with a fatal illness. As he lay dying, one of those at his bedside spoke of the good that he had done for Athens.

"What you praise in my life," he said, "has been due to fortune. I deserve no credit for it. That of which I am proudest is that no Athenian ever wore mourning because of anything done by me."

The Golden age of Pericles

His death occurred in the third year of the Peloponnesian War. It was a sad blow to the Athenians, for he was the greatest of all their statesmen.

Part II

One of the friends of Pericles was Phid´i-as, the sculptor who molded the bronze figure of Athena that stood in front of the Parthenon. He also carved the ivory and gold statue of the goddess that was inside the building.

His fame spread over all Greece, and he was invited to adorn the temple of Zeus at Olympia. For this temple he made his masterpiece. It represented Zeus seated upon his throne. The statue was so perfect that it was considered one of the wonders of the world.

When Phidias, after several years absence, returned to Athens, he was persecuted by the enemies of Pericles, because he was known to be a friend of that great statesman. He was first accused of having stolen part of the gold that had been supplied by the city to decorate the statue of Athena. Fortunately, when Phidias was working on the statue, Pericles had advised him to fasten the gold on in such a way that at any time it could be taken off and weighed. It was now removed and weighed, and the weight was found to be exactly what it should have been.

Phidias was then charged with having insulted the goddess Athena, because he had carved a likeness of himself and another of Pericles on her shield. On this charge he was cast into prison to await trial.

Before the day of the trial came, however, the great sculptor was taken sick and died.

Part III

Under Pericles Athens was at the height of her glory. The twenty-eight years during which he was at the head of Athenian affairs are known in history as the "Golden Age of Pericles." At no other time were there in Athens so many great painters, sculptors, writers, and philosophers.

A celebrated historian, who lived during the age of Pericles, was He-rod´o-tus. He is called "the Father of History."

Another famous historian of those days was Thu-cyd´i-des, who wrote a history of the Peloponnesian War.

Pericles in the Parthenon

Chapter XIX

ALCIBIADES

Part I

During the "Age of Pericles" a young man named Al-ci-bi´a-des attracted a great deal of attention in Athens. He was a kinsman of Pericles and was rich and handsome. But besides his money and his good looks there was another thing that made the people of Athens think a great deal of him. He had won the crown three times in the chariot races at the Olympic games.

These games are said to have been established by Hercules. They consisted of boxing, wrestling, running, throwing the javelin, and horse racing, and were held once in every four years in the valley of Olympia, in the little Greek state called Elis, which lay northwest of Sparta. They were so important that the Greeks reckoned time from the first Olympic games in the same way that we reckon time from the birth of Christ. These games first took place in 776 B.C. The four years from one celebration to another were called an "Olympiad."

None but Greeks might take part in the Olympic games, and while the contests were going on, tens of thousands of Greeks from every part of Hellas watched and applauded. To win the prize in any of the contests was the greatest honor for which a Greek could hope. The victor's name and the name of his birthplace were called aloud by a herald, and before the vast assemblage he was crowned with a wreath of wild olive cut with a golden knife from the sacred grove said to have been planted by Hercules.

His victories in the Olympic games made Alcibiades the idol of the Athenians. The young men of Athens admired him so much that some of them dressed as he did and even imitated his lisp. Unfortunately, he had very bad faults. He was frivolous and thoughtless, and insincere. He was, in fact, the leader of Athenian fops.

While talking with Socrates, who was very fond of him, he could talk as if he were good, or at least wished to be. But the next day he might be leading his companions into all kinds of mischief. Yet with all his faults, he was a brilliant genius. Even serious people admired him and often took his advice.

During the Peloponnesian War he persuaded the Athenians to undertake an expedition against the island of Sicily. He reminded them that Syracuse, the most important city of the island, was an ally of Sparta and an enemy of Athens. This was one reason he gave why the expedition should be undertaken. Another reason was the advantage that would come to Athens if she should add this fertile island to her possessions.

An old Athenian general named Nic´i-as opposed the expedition, but Alcibiades had his way. Ships and men were made ready and were put under three commanders — Nicias, Alcibiades, and a man named La-ma´-chus.

One morning, shortly before the fleet was to set sail, it was discovered that a shocking insult had been offered to one of the gods. Along the streets of Athens, along the country roads, and in front of the houses were busts of Hermes, who was the protector of travelers. Ears and noses had been chipped from these busts in the night. The Athenians were a very religious people, and this insult to the god filled them with terror. All feared that Hermes would punish them by not protecting people walking on the streets and highways.

Many thought Alcibiades had chipped the busts for a frolic. Soon after the fleet reached Sicily orders were received that he should return to Athens at once to answer the charge. Of course he had to give up his command.

After he did so, one disaster after another befell the expedition. The fleet entered the harbor of Syracuse. The Syracusans then blocked the entrance so that the Athenian ships could not get out. In the battle that followed, half of Nicias' ships were destroyed. Nicias ran the rest ashore and tried to escape by land, but all were forced to surrender. The old commander was killed, and those of his men who did not die in battle or of starvation were sold into slavery. Not one of the ships of the fleet ever got back to Athens.

Part II

Alcibiades was either afraid that he could not clear himself, or that he could not get justice in the courts of Athens. He therefore pretended that he was going to obey the order for his return, but instead of doing so he went for refuge to Sparta. When the Athenians heard of this they passed a sentence of death upon him.

In Sparta he was warmly welcomed and by his pleasing ways became a general favorite. The Spartans, however, soon grew suspicious of him and ordered him to be put to death as a traitor to them. He managed to escape and went to Persia. Here again, as at Athens and at Sparta, he made the people fond of him. But after a while the Persian governor, who had been his best friend, saw that he was treacherous and put him in prison. He escaped and went to a place on the Hellespont where he joined the Athenian fleet. There he gave the commanders such advice that they gained a victory over the fleet of the Spartans and the land forces of the Persians. The Spartan admiral was killed. His successor wrote to Sparta, "Our glory is gone. The men are without food. We know not what to do."

Alcibiades now thought that he might venture to go back to Athens. Because he had given advice to the commanders of the Athenian navy which had helped them defeat the Spartan fleet, the Athenians repented of having condemned him to death. So when he arrived in the Piraeus, with a small fleet of twenty vessels, he was allowed to land and go to Athens. In a very short time, he persuaded the Athenians to give him command of their fleet. Then he sailed across the Aegean to fight against the Persians and the Spartans.

Unfortunately, he had to leave the fleet for a short time. During his absence his lieutenant foolishly brought on a battle. The Athenians were defeated, and many of their ships were captured by the Spartans.

With what was left of his fleet, Alcibiades then did the strangest thing possible. He attacked a city that was friendly to the Athenians and tried to make slaves of the inhabitants. Complaint was made of this to Athens, and the Athenians at once dismissed Alcibiades from the command of their fleet.

After this he lived for some years in Asia Minor, where he owned a castle. One night his castle was surrounded by armed men who set it on fire. He ran through the flames and tried to escape, but his enemies killed him (404 B.C.).

Chapter **XX**

LYSANDER

The admiral of the Spartan fleet in the last years of the Peloponnesian War was a man named Ly-san´der. He was brave, but he was also cunning. He frequently gained the victory by laying a trap for his enemy. It is said that he used to tell his officers, "When the lion's skin is too short, you must patch it with that of a fox." This was another way of telling them that they should try to succeed by cunning when force failed.

After Alcibiades had been dismissed from the command of the Athenian fleet, a commander named Ko´non was appointed to succeed him. Lysander decided to set a trap for him. The two fleets came in sight of each other off the shore of Hellespont, near a place called Ae´gos Pot´a-mos, which means Goat's River. One morning, at the break of day, Lysander drew up his ships in line as though he intended to give battle. Later in the day the Athenians rowed toward the Spartans and challenged them to fight, but not a Spartan vessel moved. The Athenians concluded from this that the Spartans were either not prepared to fight, or were afraid. The next day the challenge was repeated, but the Spartans paid no attention to it. The same thing happened the third day and the fourth. By this time the Athenians felt sure that Lysander was afraid of them. Many therefore went on ashore, some to sleep. Only a small guard was left with the fleet.

As soon as Lysander saw that the Athenian ships were unprotected, he rowed swiftly to the place where they were lying and captured nearly the whole fleet.

One of the vessels that escaped rowed directly to Piraeus to carry the terrible news. Of one hundred and eighty ships, only about ten escaped. Three or four thousand men were taken prisoner, and all were put to death.

It arrived at night, and a sadder night was never known in Athens. The news spread through the city. Every house became a house of mourning. Nobody slept. All feared that Lysander would sail into the harbor with his victorious fleet. This was exactly what he did. All the seaports of Athens were blockaded by the Spartan vessels. The wheat supply was cut off so that the people of the city were soon half starving.

The Athenians had now neither army nor fleet. After a three month's siege, during part of which time there was a severe famine, the city surrendered.

The only hope of the citizens was that their conquerors might be generous. But in this they were disappointed. The Spartans' terms were hard and cruel. One mile of each of the Long Walls was to be pulled down. Athens was to have no larger fleet than twelve ships of war. The Spartans were to name her rulers.

To wound the pride of Athens as much as possible, Lysander had the Long Walls pulled down to the sound of music. Part of the work was done on the anniversary of the battle of Salamis, a day always celebrated in Athens in memory of her great victory over the Persians.

Thus ended the Peloponnesian War (404 B.C.). It had been a fierce struggle, and all Greece had suffered. Thucydides, who wrote the history of this war, says that never had so many cities been made desolate, never had there been such scenes of slaughter.

Athens was ruined. She had lost her ships and her army, and she was helpless in the hands of Sparta. Thirty men were appointed by the Spartans to govern the city. They are known in history as the "Thirty Tyrants." Their rule was very harsh. They allowed only 3,000 Athenians to live in Athens. The rest of the people had to leave the city, and Sparta forbade all other Grecian cities to give them refuge. Thebes and Argos, however, boldly defied this cruel order, and many of the banished Athenians went to live in these cities.

After eight months the Athenians, under a leader named Thra-sy-bu´lus, overthrew the "Tyrants." But in that short time no less than fourteen hundred Athenian citizens had been put to death.

Lysander's capture of Athens made him so popular in Sparta that for some years he was the head of the government, and he made up his mind to seize the throne.

Before he could carry out his plans, however, he was put at the head of a Spartan force and sent to the city of Thebes, against which the Spartans had declared war. His army was routed by the Thebans, and Lysander, himself, was among the slain.

Chapter XXI

SOCRATES

Part I

During the Peloponnesian War a very curious man lived in Athens. His name was Soc´ra-tes. He must have been the ugliest person in all Greece. His nose was flat, his lips were thick, his eyes were bulging, and his face was like a comic mask; yet he is thought by many to have been one of the best and wisest men that ever lived. His father was a sculptor who carved beautiful figures out of marble. When he was a boy, Socrates helped him and learned the art.

When the Spartans sent their armies to burn the farm houses of Attica and capture cities that were friendly to Athens, many of the young men of the city went forth to fight for their country. Socrates laid down his hammer and chisel and took up a shield and a spear instead. He fought in several battles, and Athens had no braver soldier. Once in winter he was ordered to a country called Thrace. It was very cold and camping out was not pleasant. However, Socrates bore the cold cheerfully, although he went barefoot and wore the same clothes that he had worn in the warm weather in Athens.

After serving as a soldier for several years, he left the army and went home to Athens. Here he became a teacher. He had no school house. His school was wherever he met persons who were willing to listen to him. It might be in the marketplace or at the street corners. On a hot summer day he would go to the harbor of Athens and chat with people who were sitting there in the shade, enjoying the cool sea breeze. He talked to the young as well as the old, and often he might be seen with a crowd of children around him. The

Socrates teaching young Alciblades

lessons that he gave were simple talks about the best way of living. This is what the Greeks called "philosophy." (The word philosophy means love of wisdom.)

Socrates was very unlike other teachers in Athens — and almost everywhere else — for he never charged his students anything for his teaching. This kept him poor. His clothes were often threadbare and shabby, and so were those of his wife Xan-thip´pe. He cared nothing for this; but she did, and it is said that she often scolded Socrates because he did nothing to make money. She felt he idled away his time in talking. Once, when he was going out of the house to escape from a severe scolding, she threw a pitcher of water upon his head. "I have often noticed, Xanthippe, that rain comes after thunder," said the philosopher.

No man ever had better friends than Socrates. But no man ever had worse enemies. Some people disliked him because he asked them questions which they could not answer without admitting that they were very foolish in their way of living. Others said that he was teaching people not to worship Zeus and Athena and the other gods of Athens. They said he was misleading the young men of the city.

One of his enemies was a poet called Ar-i-stoph´a-nes, who is famous for his comic plays. In one of them a wild young man is one of the characters and Socrates is another. Aristophanes made it seem that the teachings of Socrates had caused the young man to become wild. The play did Socrates a great deal of harm, for many people came to believe that he really was advising young men to lead bad lives.

Yet one of the worst young men of Athens once said, "You think that I have no shame in me, but when I am with Socrates I am ashamed. He has only to speak and my tears flow."

Finally, the enemies of Socrates brought him to court. They charged him with ruining the young men and insulting the gods. He was tried and condemned to drink the deadly juice of a plant called hemlock. In Athens condemned persons were usually put to death by making them drink this poison.

Socrates received the unjust sentence grandly. Before he left the court he said, "My judges, you go now to your homes — I to prison and death. But which of the two is the better lot God only knows. It is very likely that death is our greatest blessing."

Generally, a person condemned to death had to drink the poison the very next day after his trial. But a sacred ship had just sailed from Athens to De´los. Every year the ship carried the offerings of the Athenians to Apollo, the chief god of the island. The law of Athens said that no person condemned to die

The school of Plato

should be put to death while the ship was travelling to and from Delos. So for thirty days Socrates was kept in prison.

During that time his friends were allowed to go to see him. In the prison he talked to them just as he had done in the market place or on the streets.

Some of his friends told him how sorry they were that he should die innocent.

"What!" said Socrates, "would you have me die guilty?"

On the return of the ship from Delos he was told to prepare himself for death. He invited his friends to come and be with him at the end. He ate his last meal with them, and was as cheerful during it as if it had been a feast.

One of the friends asked where he would like them to bury him.

"Bury **me**?" he said. "You cannot bury Socrates. You can bury my body; you cannot put **me** into a grave."

He spoke about death and the future life and said that death was only the end of sorrow and the beginning of a nobler life.

When the jailer came with the cup of poison, Socrates drank it cheerfully as if it had been a glass of wine. He walked around the cell as he was bidden and then, beginning to feel sleepy, lay down. Soon after this he stopped breathing.

Pla´to, who was one of his pupils, says, "Thus died the man who was in death the noblest we have ever known — in life, the wisest and the best."

The death of Socrates

Part II

After the death of Socrates (399 B.C.) his work was carried on by his pupil, Plato. Plato became one of the most famous philosophers of Greece. His lectures were given in the shade of the trees planted by Cimon in the Academy years before.

Besides great philosophers, Athens had some famous painters. Two of the most celebrated were Zeux´is and Par-rha´si-us, who lived about 400 B.C. They were rivals. Once they gave an exhibition of their paintings. Zeuxis exhibited a bunch of grapes which had such a natural look that the birds came and pecked at them. The people exclaimed, "Astonishing! What can be finer than Zeuxis' grapes?"

Zeuxis proudly turned to his rival's picture. A purple curtain hung before it. "Draw aside your curtain, Parrhasius," he said, "and let us look at your picture."

The artist smiled, but did not move. Some one else stepped toward the curtain to draw it aside, and it was then discovered that the curtain was part of the painting.

"I yield," said Zeuxis. "It is easy to see who is the better artist. I have deceived birds. Parrhasius has deceived an artist."

It is said that Zeuxis died of laughing at a funny picture that he had painted of an old woman.

98

Chapter XXII

XENOPHON

Part I

One day as Socrates was walking through a narrow street in Athens, he met a young man who was remarkably handsome. Socrates stretched out his staff so that the young man had to stop.

"Where can bread be found?" asked the philosopher.

The young man's manner was modest and pleasing as he told Socrates where to buy bread.

"And where can wine be found?" asked the philosopher.

With the same pleasant manner, the young man told Socrates where to get wine.

"And where can the good and the noble be found?" asked the philosopher.

The young man was puzzled and unable to answer.

"Follow me and learn," said the philosopher. The young man obeyed and from that time forward he was the pupil and friend of Socrates. He was called Xen´o-phon, a name that afterward became famous among the Greeks.

The king of Persia at that time was Ar´ta-xerx´es. He had a younger brother named Cyrus, who was the governor of some provinces of Asia Minor, which belonged to Persia. Cyrus thought that he had a better right to the throne than Artaxerxes and he determined to seize it.

The Persians had helped the Spartans in the Peloponnesian War, and Cyrus had found out what splendid fighters the Greeks were. He knew, also, that many of them had become so used to fighting that they did not like a life of peace and were willing to fight for anyone who would pay them. He decided, therefore, to get the Greeks to help him to fight for the throne of Persia. He sent to several Greek states to invite soldiers to join him, promising them great rewards if he succeeded.

Xenophon had a friend who was going with Cyrus and who advised Xenophon to go too. Xenophon talked the matter over with Socrates who told him to ask the oracle at Delphi what to do. So Xenophon went to Delphi, but as he had made up his mind to go on the expedition, he did not ask the oracle whether he should go or not. He only asked to what gods he should sacrifice before he set out. After sacrificing as the oracle advised, he started for Sardis, in Asia Minor, and reached that city just in time to join the expedition.

Eleven thousand Greeks from different states had entered the service of Cyrus; so that with the Persian forces, 100,000 strong, he had an army of 111,000 men. Xenophon was not a general, or even a soldier, in this army. He seems to have gone with his friend, hoping that some opening would be made for him.

There was a magnificent road from Sardis, Artaxerxes' capital city. But even upon the best roads, an army of a hundred thousand men, most of whom were on foot, had to move slowly. Cyrus' troops went about fifteen miles a day, and it took them about six months to reach a place called Cu-nax´a, about seventy miles from Bab´y-lon.

Here they found Artaxerxes at the head of an army of nearly a million men. The troops of the Persian king advanced with a great shout, thinking that the noise made by thousands of men shouting would terrify the Greeks. But the Greeks only raised their usual war cry, "Victory!" They steadily advanced, overcoming everything that was opposed to them. Unfortunately, Cyrus went into the battle himself at the head of his Persian forces. Seeing his brother, he rushed forward, exclaiming, "I see the man." He wounded Artaxerxes with a javelin.

He, himself, was quickly killed by the soldiers of Artaxerxes. As soon as their leader had fallen, Cyrus' Persian soldiers lost heart and fled.

Part II

The Greeks were now in a terrible plight. They were six month's march from Sardis and opposed by an army a hundred times the size of their own.

In the battle of Cunaxa they had so thoroughly beaten the Persians that Artaxerxes and his men were afraid of them and decided to get rid of them by treachery. The Persian commander-in-chief, Tis-sa-pher´nes, therefore invited the Greek generals to a friendly meeting and promised to furnish them guides and provisions, so that they might return safely to Greece. The generals, never suspecting foul play, went to the Persian camp. There they were all put to death.

The Greeks were now greatly alarmed. The night following the assassination of the generals was one of terror. Not a fire was lit, not even for cooking supper. All slept with their weapons at their sides while the sentries listened to catch the slightest sound.

Xenophon spent the night in thinking what was best to do. It was clear to him that someone must be chosen by the Greeks as their leader and that they all must stand by one another. He felt sure that if this were done, there would be a good chance of getting home safely. In the morning he told his thoughts and hopes to others of the Greeks, who were greatly cheered by what he said. Although he had held no office in the army before, he was now made one of its generals.

The shortest way to get out of the kingdom of Persia was to go to the Euxine, now called the Black Sea, which lay many hundreds of miles to the north beyond rugged mountains. At one of the ports on the shore of that sea, the Greeks hoped to find ships in which they might sail to Greece.

The march was begun at once. All sorts of hardships were met with. There were snow-storms and bitter north winds. It was sometimes hard to get enough food. The mountain tribes, through whose land the army had to march, were often unfriendly and rolled rocks down the mountain slopes upon the soldiers.

At last, however, they reached the shores of the Euxine. Since the murder of their generals, the Greeks had marched for five months in an enemy's territory. They had drawn supplies from the country and had lost but a few of their men. The retreat was, in fact, a victory.

Xenophon returned to Greece, but he did not go back to Athens. During some of the time that he had followed a soldier's fortune, he had fought with the Spartans against Athens and the Athenians had passed a sentence of exile against him.

He went to Sparta, and soon afterward settled on an estate in Elis. "Xenophon's farm" is still pointed out to visitors in Greece. He passed about twenty years quietly in hunting, writing, and entertaining his friends with stories of his life as a soldier on faraway battlefields.

From notes which he made, he wrote a history called the A-nab´a-sis, or "March up" which is an account of Cyrus' march up to Babylon and of the retreat of the Greeks.

Because of political troubles, Xenophon finally had to leave his pleasant home in Elis. He went to Corinth, where it is supposed that he died.

Chapter XXIII

EPAMINONDAS AND PELOPIDAS

Part I

In the city of Thebes, not long after the Peloponnesian War, there lived two men whose names were Pe-lop´i-das and E-pam-i-non´das. Pelopidas was rich; Epaminondas was poor. Both were fond of athletics and manly sports, but Epaminondas found his chief pleasure in books. Both were brave men and true, and they loved each other like brothers.

Once, when their city was an ally of Sparta, they were sent by Thebes as soldiers to help the Spartans in a war with their neighbors, the Arcadians. The young men were fighting side by side when their comrades gave way and fled. Closing their shields together, they bravely held their ground and tried to drive back the Arcadians. Pelopidas was wounded and fell. Epaminondas would not desert his friend. Although badly wounded, he held the Arcadians in check until help came, and he and Pelopidas were rescued.

In time, Sparta became jealous of Thebes and tried to take away the liberty of her people. A few rich Thebans were willing to help Sparta do this in hopes that they might be made the rulers. One day they led a band of Spartan soldiers, who happened to be passing, into the Cad-me´a. This was the rocky citadel of Thebes which rose above the city as the Acropolis rose above Athens. But on that day the garrison was taking a holiday, for the citadel had been given up to the women who were celebrating a festival of Demeter in it. The Spartans easily took possession of it. Having once won it, they held it for four years. During that time the men who had betrayed the citadel into Spartan hands ruled Thebes as tyrants. They put some of the Thebans to death and banished others. Over three

Epaminondas rescues Pelopidas

hundred Thebans were sent away. Among the banished was Pelopidas. Epaminondas was so poor that the tyrants did not think him of any consequence, and he was allowed to stay in Thebes. He used his influence to get the young Thebans to drill in order to make themselves superior to the Spartans in skill and strength.

Part II

The exiles went to Athens. After living there for a few years, Pelopidas determined to free his country. He easily persuaded the other exiles and some Athenians to join in carring out his plans.

When everything was ready, the exiles left Athens. Twelve of them volunteered to get into Thebes and kill the tyrants. They disguised themselves as hunters, divided into four parties, and taking hounds with them, hunted through the fields around Thebes. As dusk came on they made their way into the city. It was a cold winter day. Snow was beginning to fall, and because very few people were in the streets, the exiles reached the house where all were to meet without being noticed. Twenty-six citizens joined them, and all remained in the one house until near midnight.

A patriot who was in the plot had invited the tyrants to supper at his house. As, the supper wine was served, the tyrants drank freely. After the supper, some of the patriots, dressed as women, were admitted to the banquet hall. As soon as they entered the room the guests greeted them warmly. The supposed women at once threw off their veils, drew their swords and killed the tyrants.

Pelopidas, with another party, went to the houses of two of the tyrants who had refused the invitation to supper, and after a fight, killed them. The patriots then went from house to house, calling on all the people to defend their homes. The Spartan soldiers in the Cadmea heard the noise and saw the lights, but were afraid to come out.

In the morning the other exiles, with friends from Athens came into the city, and all the citizens rose up in arms. The Spartan garrison gave up the Cadmea, and Thebes was free.

Part III

Sparta waited eight years before a chance came to punish the Thebans. Then war was declared, and an army of ten thousand Spartans marched against Thebes.

The Thebans also raised an army, and through the influence of Pelopidas, Epaminondas was elected one of the chief captains. Pelopidas himself was the captain of a famous sacred band of three hundred young men who had taken oaths to give their lives in defense of liberty.

The two armies met near a town called Le-ne´tra. There Epaminondas gained a great victory, although his army was less than half as large as that of the Spartans.

Epaminondas and Pelopidas drilled the men of Thebes so that they were the best soldiers in all Greece. Thebes helped other Greek cities become independent.

Pelopidas went to Thessaly to aid the people of that state against a tyrant who was trying to rule all Thessaly. The army of Pelopidas was not nearly so large as that of the tyrant, but Pelopidas was victorious. Unfortunately, he was killed in the battle.

The Thessalians begged the Thebans to allow them to bury the hero, and their request was granted.

Part IV

The death of Pelopidas was a sad blow to Epaminondas, but he did not let his grief stand in the way of duty. Athens at this time had grown jealous of Thebes and had united with Sparta. The armies of the two cities met the Thebans under Epaminondas in the year 362 B.C., near the town of Man-ti-ne´a, where a long and fierce battle was fought. At length the Thebans were victorious, and the Spartans were driven from the field.

The victory, however, was dearly bought. Just when the tide of battle was turning and the Spartan ranks were breaking, Epaminondas received a wound in the breast from a spear. The shaft broke and the head remained fixed in the wound. Epaminondas was told by his physician that he would die as soon as the spear head was removed. Those about him wept, and one lamented that he was dying without a child to keep his name alive.

"Leuctra and Mantinea," replied the hero, "are daughters who will keep my name alive."

When he was told that the victory was secure he cried, "I have lived long enough," and with his own hand drew the head of the spear from his breast.

Chapter XXIV

PHILIP OF MACEDONIA

Part I

After the death of Epaminondas, Thebes soon lost the high place she had gained among the states of Greece. For a while no state held that place. Sparta was never powerful after her defeats at Leuctra and Mantinea. And although Athens had rebuilt her Long Walls, she was not the strong power that she had once been.

A state, partly Greek and partly barbarian, lying far to the north, suddenly took the lead in the affairs of Greece. This state was Macedonia.

The king of Macedonia had a brother named Philip who had spent a part of his youth in Thebes. He had seen Thebes become the greatest of Grecian states through the bravery and military skill of Epaminondas, and he determined to make his own state great.

The chance came to carry out his determination. The king of Macedonia was assassinated, and the brother who succeeded him was killed in battle. Philip's infant nephew was heir to the throne, and Philip became the guardian of the little king. In a short time the claims of his nephew had been set aside, and Philip was on the throne of Macedonia.

Not long after he became king, Philip was married to O-lym´pi-as, a proud and beautiful woman, daughter of the king of E-pi´rus. Philip had seen her for the first time at a feast of the Dyonisus, the god of wine. She and her maidens were dancing among garlands of vines and flowers. On the head of Olympias was an ivy crown, and in her hand a staff twined with a vine branch. As she danced, her wild beauty won the heart of Philip. He asked for her hand in marriage, and she became his wife.

Philip soon showed that he was a wise ruler. He treated his people with fairness, and they became very fond of him.

One day, after he had been drinking, he was acting as a judge and gave a decision against a woman. His sentence seemed so unfair to her that she thought he was under the influence of liquor. "I appeal," she cried.

"I am the king. To whom do you appeal?" asked Philip.

"I appeal from Philip drunk to Philip sober," she replied. The next day Philip considered her case again and decided in her favor.

Part II

It was, however, his skill as a soldier that most endeared Philip to his people. He knew that the Spartans had become the masters of Greece because every Spartan was a trained soldier. He knew that Epaminondas had won his great battles because of the way in which he arranged his men. Philip, therefore, had his army carefully drilled, and in battle he arranged his soldiers in his famous phalanx.

This phalanx consisted of a mass of men, sixteen deep. If there were 16,000 men, the front rank had 1,000 men standing side by side. Three feet behind these stood a second rank of 1,000. Behind the second rank stood a third line of 1,000 equally close, and so on until there was a solid body of men sixteen deep and a thousand wide. Every man bore a round shield, about two feet in diameter, and a spike or spear, twenty one feet long. The shields were buckled to the left arm and were held close together. Before them bristled the spear points like a hedge. Against these spear points neither men nor horses could advance, and the charge of the phalanx broke down everything before it.

Athens and Thebes were finally aroused to action against Philip by the eloquence of De-mos´the-nes, the great orator, who was constantly sounding a warning. An army was sent to oppose the Macedonian. Philip met this army at Chae-ro-ne´a, not far from Thebes, and there gained a great victory.

This put an end to the power of Athens and Thebes and made Philip master of all the states of Greece, except Sparta.

But Philip was wise enough and fair enough not to become a tyrant. He knew the history of Sparta. The military training of the Spartans had made them strong. Their tyranny had made them weak, for no state of Greece was ever content to remain under Spartan rule. Philip, therefore, acted generously toward the conquered states. He let each manage its own affairs, while a General Council, like our Congress, managed matters in which all were concerned.

The first thing that Philip proposed to the Council of the States was that all of Greece should make war against Persia. The members of the Council were delighted and Philip was invited to be the commander-in-chief of the expedition.

Preparations for the invasion of Persia had already begun when Philip's career was suddenly ended by an assassin. The assassin approached the king at a wedding feast, and suddenly plunged a sword into his body, killing him.

See pg 56 in Kingfisher

Chapter **XXV**

ALEXANDER THE GREAT

Part I

Young Alexander was educated by Aristotle.

Alexander, the son of Philip of Macedonia and Olympias, was born on the same night that the great temple of Diana at Eph´e-sus, in Asia Minor, was burned. It is said that while the temple was burning, the soothsayers ran up and down the streets of Ephesus, crying out that the night had brought forth sad disaster to Asia. This was true of the birth of Alexander as well as of the burning of the temple.

Alexander was educated chiefly by the famous Greek philosopher, Aristotle. The young prince was an earnest pupil. It is said that he could recite the **Iliad** of Homer from beginning to end.

He excelled also in athletic sports. The horses of Thessaly, a state of Greece adjoining Macedonia, were famed for their speed and spirit. While Alexander was still a boy, a fine Thessalian horse was offered to his father at a very high price. Philip wished to have the animal tried, but the horse was so wild that everyone was afraid of him. Philip was about to send him away when Alexander offered to ride him. The king gave him permission. Alexander had noticed that the animal was afraid of his own shadow. He, therefore, seized the plunging horse and turned his head toward the sun, so that his shadow fell behind him.

Alexander tames Bucephalus

Then patting his neck and speaking gently to him, he leaped upon his back and soon completely tamed him.

The head of the horse was supposed to have some likeness to that of an ox, so he was called Bu-ceph´a-lus, or Oxhead. He became Alexander's favorite horse and carried his master through many a march and many a battle.

Alexander's ambition was shown at an early age. While he was yet a mere boy, he made up his mind to conquer the world. When he learned from Aristotle that there were many other worlds in the universe, he was greatly saddened by the thought that he had not yet conquered one.

As Philip went on making one conquest after another, Alexander became alarmed. "Why," he cried one day, "my father will leave nothing for me to do!"

However, when he became king, he found enough to do. First of all there were other claimants to the throne besides himself. Some of them Alexander put to death. Others fled the country. He learned that Thebes and other Greek states were thinking of throwing off the Macedonian yoke. Therefore, he gathered a large army and marched to Thebes at the head of it. The Thebans were overawed and submitted to him without resistance. The Athenians, in spite of Demosthenes' advice, sent a messenger to him while he was at Thebes, offering their submission. A little later the Greeks met in general council at Corinth and gave him, as they had given Philip, the command of the expedition that was to be undertaken against Persia. Sparta alone refused to agree in the vote.

Alexander returned to Macedonia and marched against some Thracian tribes in the northern part of his dominions. While he was subduing them a report of his death reached Greece, and Thebes again took up arms. Suddenly Alexander appeared in Greece with his victorious army. He took Thebes by assault and pulled to the ground every building in the city except the house once occupied by the famous poet Pindar. Six thousand of the inhabitants were put to death; a few escaped by flight and the rest were sold as slaves.

Map of Alexander's world

Part II

Alexander now began to prepare for the great expedition against Persia, which had been so long planned. Soon his army was ready to march. It consisted of less than 35,000 men, but with these he boldly crossed the Hellespont.

He landed on the Asiatic coast not far from the site of ancient Troy. From the plain of Troy he marched to the river Gra-ni´cus where he fought his first battle with the Persians.

The Persian army was completely routed, and its commander killed himself rather than face the disgrace of his defeat. The great city of Sardis, the stronghold of the Persians in western Asia Minor, now opened its gates to the conqueror.

The following spring, Alexander advanced into the province of Phryg´i-a. In a temple in the city of Gor´di-um, the chariot of Gor´di-us, a famous Phrygian king, was kept. The yoke of the chariot was fastened to the pole by a knot of tough fiber. The knot was said to have been tied by Gordius himself. It was very puzzling. An oracle had declared that whoever should untie the knot would become the master of Asia. Instead of trying to untie it, Alexander cut it with one stroke of his sword. The people of Asia Minor took this as an omen that he was to be their master and offered him but little resistance.

Beyond the mountains in southeastern Asia Minor, the "Great King," Darius was waiting for the Greeks with an enormous army. He became impatient and crossed the mountains into Ci-lic´i-a. A battle was fought at Is´sus, but the Persians were no match for the Greeks. The battle ended with overwhelming defeat to the army of Darius, and he fled from the battlefield. He left not only his baggage and treasure, but his wife, his mother, and his children, all of whom fell into Alexander's hands. These captives were treated with much respect and kindness by the conqueror.

Soon after the battle at Issus, Damascus was captured. Alexander then moved against Tyre, a famous port of Syria, whose trade was with every land and whose merchants were princes. So great were the resources of the city that it withstood a siege of seven months. At the end of that time it fell into Alexander's hands, and thirty thousand of its citizens were captured and made slaves.

From Tyre, Alexander marched toward Egypt. On the way he passed through the Holy Land. When he reached Jerusalem, he was met by a friendly procession of priests and Levites. They came out from the gates of the city, with the high priest at their head, to bid the conqueror welcome.

Egypt, like the Holy Land, was won without a battle. The people were weary of Persian rule.

In Egypt, Alexander founded a city near the mouth of the Nile which he hoped would be a great trading port. It is still called Alexandria after its founder. Alexander extended a special invitation to the Jews to settle in his new city. The Jewish community in Alexandria prospered and became an important center of learning and scholarship. It was in Alexandria that seventy learned Jewish scholars completed the translation of the books of the **Old Testament** from Hebrew into Greek. This translation is called the **Septuagint** (from the Greek word for seventy) and became the basis for many subsequent translations of the Old Testament into other languages.

In the spring of the year 331 B.C., Alexander again set out in pursuit of Darius, who had now collected another large army.

In October, not far from a place called Ar-be´la, in Persia, the forces of Darius and Alexander met in their last great battle. Darius had done everything he could to insure the defeat of the Greeks. His army was said to number one million men. One division of it had two hundred chariots, and to their wheels, scythes were attached. The scythes went round with the wheels and were expected to mow down the Greeks like grass. In another division of the army were fifteen trained elephants that were intended to rush wildly among the Greeks and trample them down.

But the scythe-armed chariots, the elephants, and the million men were all unsuccessful. The vast host was completely routed, and Darius turned his chariot and fled.

The family of Darius at Alexander's feet

From Arbela, Alexander pushed on to Bab´y-lon, whose brazen gates were thrown open to him. Su´sa, another great city of the Empire, surrendered without resistance. Then to make his conquest complete he marched on to Per-sep´o-lis, the magnificent capital of Persia, itself. This city, with its immense treasure of silver and gold, fell into his hands. Five thousand camels and ten thousand mule carts carried away the spoils, the value of which is said to have been $150,000,000.

Alexander pursued Darius, but before he overtook him, the Great King was murdered by one of his own satraps. Alexander had the body buried with royal honors and punished the satrap with death.

The Empire of Persia now lay at Alexander's feet, and the work for which the expedition had set out was finished. The young king, however, had no desire to return to Macedonia. He had conquered the East, but the East had also conquered him. He had become a slave to its ways of living. His old simple Macedonian tastes had been laid aside, and his life was given up to pleasure.

Part III

Soon, he undertook another conquest and at the head of his veteran soldiers advanced eastward into Bac´tri-a and added this province to his dominions. Among the Bactrian captives was a beautiful princess named Roxana, who became his bride.

Southeast of Persia lay India, a vast empire, rich in gold and diamonds. Alexander desired to add it to his conquests.

Porus before Alexander

Great mountain ranges enclose India on the north and northwest. Crossing these are passes, through which travelers from Central Asia must go to reach India.

Alexander went by the way of the Khy´ber Pass and marched steadily onward until he reached the River Hy-das´pes. There an Indian king, named Po´rus, engaged him in battle. Porus proved to be the most desperate fighter Alexander had met in all Asia. When the Indian was at length overpowered, captured, and brought before the conqueror, Alexander asked him how he expected to be treated.

"Like a king," replied Porus.

"That you certainly shall be," said Alexander. And so he was, for it was the habit of Alexander to treat all whom he conquered honorably.

On the bank of the River Hydaspes, Alexander lost his horse Bucephalus. There, at the place where the animal died, Alexander founded a city which he named Bu-ceph´a-la in honor of his favorite horse.

The conqueror was not able to go on with his Indian campaign. His soldiers were worn out with marching and fighting and insisted that they would go no farther. And so, much against his will, Alexander was obliged to lead them back to Persia.

The return march was one of great hardship. At the mouth of the In´dus, Alexander sent the fleet to sail along the coast and up the Persian Gulf, while he led the land forces

The death of Alexander

toward Susa and Babylon. The army had to march through a country which was hot, dry and barren. The men suffered dreadfully, and Alexander shared their sufferings.

Shortly after reaching Babylon, he was attacked by a fever, which he did not have the strength to resist.

His generals gathered around his death bed. They asked him to name the one who was to succeed him. Alexander drew his signet ring from his finger, and handed it to Per-dic´cas saying, "To the strongest." A little later, he stopped breathing.

Thus passed away one of the greatest soldiers the world has ever known. At the time of his death, 323 B.C., he was only thirty-two years old. His victories had been won and his conquests had been made in the short space of twelve years.

Demosthenes practicing oratory

Skip

Chapter XXVI

DEMOSTHENES

Part I

In the city of Athens about twenty-five years after the Peloponnesian War there lived a delicate boy named Demosthenes. His father was a manufacturer of swords and made a great deal of money. But when Demosthenes was only seven years old his father died. Guardians had charge of his property for ten years. They robbed the boy of part of his fortune and managed the rest so badly that Demosthenes could not go to school under the best teachers in Athens because he did not have enough money to pay them.

One day, when he was sixteen years old, a great trial was going on at Athens, and he strolled into court. There were fifteen hundred and one dicasts or, as we call them, jurymen in their seats, and the court was crowded with citizens who, like Demosthenes has gone in from curiosity.

A lawyer named Cal-li-stra´tus was speaking. He did not finish his speech for nearly four hours, but no one left the court until he stopped talking. Then hundreds of people went out and hurried home. Demosthenes waited to see the end. When each of the jurymen had thrown a voting pebble into a basket, the clerk of the court counted the pebbles and announced the result. Callistratus had won the case.

Demosthenes went home determined to become a lawyer and public speaker. In one year from that time he brought suit against his guardians, delivered four orations against them and won his case. He recovered a large part of the property which his father had left to his mother and himself.

After this he entered public life, but the first speech he delivered in the public assembly was a complete failure. He stammered and could not speak loud enough, and in trying to do so he made odd faces.

People laughed at him, and even his friends told him that he never could be a speaker. He went home greatly cast down.

Then an actor who was a great friend of his family went to see him and encouraged him. He asked Demosthenes to read some passages of poetry to him. The actor then recited the same passages. The verses now seemed to have new meaning and beauty. The actor pronounced the words as if he felt them. The tones of his voice were clear and pleasant, and his gestures were graceful. Demosthenes was charmed.

"You can learn to speak just as well as I do," said the actor, "if you are willing to work patiently. Do not be discouraged, but conquer your difficulties."

"I will," said Demosthenes. And he did.

It is said that to improve his voice, he spoke with stones in his mouth. To become accustomed to the noise and confusion of the public assembly, he went to the seashore and recited there amid the roar of the waves. To overcome his habit of lifting one shoulder above the other he suspended a sword so that the point would prick his shoulder as he raised it.

He built an underground room where he could study without interruption and practice speaking without disturbing anyone. He had one side of his head shaved so that he would be ashamed to leave his retreat. Then he stayed there for months at a time engaged in study. One thing that he did while he was there was to copy eight times the speeches in the famous history of Thucydides. This was to teach him to use the most fitting language. In addition to all this, he took lessons from an excellent speaker named I-sae´us who taught rhetoric. In this way the awkward boy who had been laughed out of the assembly became in time the greatest orator of Athens.

Not only was Demosthenes a graceful orator, but he was wise and loved the city of Athens dearly. He soon acquired great influence in Athens and became one of the ten official orators.

At this time Philip of Macedon had organized a strong army and was beginning those conquests which were to make him master of Greece. From the first, Demosthenes regarded him with suspicion, but said nothing until he was convinced that Philip was threatening the liberty of Athens and of all Greece. Then he urged the Athenians to fight against Philip the way their forefathers had fought against the Persians at Marathon, at Salamis, and at Plataea. "Philip," he said, "is weak because he is selfish and unjust. He is strong only because he is energetic. Let us be equally energetic, and being unselfish and just, we shall triumph."

Philip's victory at Chaeronea completely disheartened the Athenians, and Demosthenes had to use all the power of his eloquence to rouse them. In his speeches he showed how the success of Philip and the failure of Athens were not due to the advisors of the people or to the generals who led their army, but to the Athenians themselves. "You idle away your time," he said, "going into barbers' shops and asking what's new today, while Philip is gathering forces with which to crush you and the rest of Greece with you."

Philip tried to bribe Demosthenes, but the orator was absolutely incorruptible. To the end of his life, he spoke out for the cause of freedom against both Philip and Alexander. He delivered twelve orations on this subject. Three of these orations were specifically directed against Philip and are known as the "Phil-ip´pics." They were so bitter in their denunciation of Philip that today any speech which is very bitter and severe against a man or a party is called a philippic.

The most famous speech that Demosthenes ever made was in defense of himself and it is known as the speech, "On the Crown." He had advised the Athenians to unite with the Thebans against Philip. His advice was followed, and a victory was won. The Athenians were so much pleased that someone proposed to crown Demosthenes with a golden wreath at one of the festivals. Now this proposal had to be voted on by the people, and some of Demosthenes' enemies objected. If the people refused to vote the crown, it would have meant disgrace for Demosthenes. He was thus obliged to go before the assembly to speak in defense of himself and to show that his advice to his countrymen had been correct. It was true that the Athenians had not been able to destroy Philip's power, or free the states of Greece from his control. "But," said Demosthenes, "I insist that even if it had been known beforehand to all the world that Philip would succeed and that we should fail, not even then ought Athens to have taken any other course if she had any regard for her own glory or for her past or for the ages to come." By this he meant that it was the duty of her people to fight for what they believed to be right even if in the very beginning they had known that they would not succeed.

When the vote was taken, the people decided that he should receive the crown.

Part II

When the news reached Athens of the murder of Philip, Demosthenes rejoiced and placed a wreath upon his head, as if he were at a feast. He even persuaded the Athenians to make a thank offering to their gods.

Alexander soon placed the Greek cities at his mercy. Then he demanded that Demosthenes and eight other Athenian orators should be delivered up to be punished for treason. Demosthenes told the people of Athens the story of the wolf and the sheep.

"Once upon a time," he said, "the shepherds agreed with the wolf that henceforth they should be friends. The wolf promised faithfully never again to attack the sheep. But he said he thought it would be only fair that the shepherds should cease to keep dogs. The shepherds agreed and gave up their dogs. Then the wolf ate up the sheep."

The Athenians knew what Demosthenes meant, and heeded the lesson. They kept their watchdogs, Demosthenes and the other orators, safely at home.

Alexander eventually withdrew his demand and treated the Athenians with kindness. However, this did not win the favor of Demosthenes, who continued to oppose the Macedonians at every step.

After some years one of Alexander's satraps stole a large treasure, fled to Athens and begged for protection. Demosthenes was unjustly accused of helping him and was condemned to pay a fine. He could not pay it and so went into exile.

When Alexander died the orator returned to Athens. The Athenians sent a man-of-war to bring him to Piraeus. The magistrates, the priests, and all the citizens marched out to welcome him and escort him to the city.

Demosthenes now made a last effort to free Athens. But Macedonia was still strong, and Athens and those who loved her were weak. In a short time the demand was again made that the orators be given up to be punished, and Demosthenes again had to flee for his life. He sought refuge in a temple of Poseidon on an island near the coast of Greece.

The sacredness of the temple ought to have protected him, but he was not allowed to escape. The captain of the soldiers who were sent to kill him told him that if he would come out of the temple, he should be pardoned. Demosthenes knew well that this promise would be broken. He asked to be allowed a few moments in which to write a letter, and his request was granted. He wrote, and then placed the end of his writing quill in his mouth. Those who were watching him saw him grow pale. He tried to reach the door, but fell dead near the altar. He had taken poison which he had long carried in the end of this writing quill, for he feared that if he ever fell into the hands of the Macedonians, he would die in prison, or by torture.

Chapter *XXVII*

ARISTOTLE, ZENO, DIOGENES AND APELLES

Part I

While Alexander was conquering the world, there lived in Athens a man whose work survived hundreds of years after the conqueror's empire fell to pieces. Indeed, it exists today. This man was Aristotle, the great philosopher, at one time Alexander's tutor.

After Alexander became king, Aristotle went to Athens and established a school of philosophy. His fame grew, and he was called "the man of wisdom." He spent much of his time writing, and wrote about almost everything that men thought of in his time. Some of his works are studied in our colleges today.

Like all other great men of Greece, Aristotle had enemies. Some of them accused him of not having respect for the gods. Because of this accusation, he fled from Athens in order, as he said, to keep the Athenians from sinning against philosophy by banishing him. He died in exile.

It is said that for about two hundred years after his death, people did not know what had happened to his writings. The men to whom they were left had buried them in an underground chamber for fear that the king of Pergamos, who was very proud of his library, would get hold of them. When the manuscripts were found, they could still be read.

For hundreds of years after that, Aristotle's writings were more widely studied in Europe than almost any other books.

Top: *Plato and Aristotle at the school in Athens*
Above: *Aristotle lecturing at the school in Athens*

Part II

Another great philosopher who lived during the time of Alexander was Zeno. He was born in Cyprus, but came to Athens in his youth.

He gave his lectures in a porch, called in Greek a Sto´a, from which he and his followers are called Sto´ics. He taught that men should live simply, and learn to be neither fond of pleasure nor cast down by sorrow. Today we call people stoics who endure pain and misfortune without complaining.

One of Zeno's rivals was a philosopher named Ep-i-cu´rus. He founded a school in Athens and taught there for thirty-six years. His enemies accused him of teaching that pleasure was the only thing to live for, and many people still have this idea. We call a man an "epicure" who is very fond of high living. Epicurus used the word pleasure to mean peace of mind, not the mere satisfaction of eating and drinking.

A reading of Homer

Both he and his pupils lived in a very simple way.

One of the oddest of the Greek philosophers was Di-og´e-nes. He used to stand in the public places of the city and ridicule the follies of his fellow citizens. Because of this habit he and his disciples were called cynics, or growlers, from a Greek word which means dog. It is said that he lived in a tub.

Many stories are told of the curious doings and sayings of Diogenes. Once, in broad daylight, he walked through the streets of Athens carrying a lighted lantern.

"What are you about now, Diogenes?" asked one who met him.

"I am looking for an honest man," sneered Diogenes.

Another time, when he was on a voyage, the ship in which he was sailing was captured by pirates. The passengers and crew were taken to Crete and sold as slaves. The auctioneer who was selling them asked Diogenes what he could do. "I can rule men," was the answer. "Sell me to someone who wishes a master."

When the great Council of States of Greece honored Alexander by asking him to

Diogenes in his tub

lead their forces against Persia, the young conqueror visited Diogenes. The philosopher was then living at Corinth, in the house of the man who had bought him as a slave. He was in the garden basking in the sun when Alexander visited him.

"Can I do anything to help you, Diogenes?" asked Alexander.

"Nothing but get out of my sunshine," replied Diogenes.

As Alexander was leaving this man of few wants, he said, "If I were not Alexander, I should wish to be Diogenes." It was as though he had said, "If I were not going to conquer the world, I should like to have the power which Diogenes has to conquer self."

Part III

A number of celebrated painters lived during the reign of Alexander. The most famous was A-pel´les. Alexander would allow no one else to paint his portrait. Apelles had talent, but he became a great artist as much by his patient industry as by his talent. His motto was "Never a day without a line."

Once he painted a horse and exhibited it in a contest with some of his rivals who also had painted pictures of horses. He saw that the judges were not going to give the prize to his picture, so he requested that all the pictures should be shown to some horses. This was done, and the animals paid no more attention to the pictures of Apelles' rivals than they would have paid to blank boards. When Apelles's horse was shown to them, it is said that they neighed as though they had seen an old friend.

Chapter XXVIII

PTOLEMY

One of Alexander's favorite generals was Ptol´e-my. In the division of the Empire, Egypt was placed in his charge. Other parts of the Empire were entrusted to other generals. One had Macedonia, another Thrace, another Syria. At first they ruled as governors for Alexander's young son, but after a while they became independent and were called kings.

Ptolemy and his descendants ruled Egypt for more than three hundred and fifty years. They were a great line of sovereigns and did much for the good of the country. We are accustomed to thinking of them as Egyptians, but really they were Greeks living in Egypt.

One of Ptolemy's first acts, and one which shows that he was a man of affectionate feeling, was to bring the body of Alexander from Babylon to Egypt. It was first buried in Memphis but afterward removed to Alexandria, because, as you remember, this city was founded by Alexander and named after him.

Ptolemy made Alexandria his capital and did a great deal to beautify the city. He founded a museum and began collecting books for a library.

His son, Ptolemy Philadelphus, carried on this work and made the library the largest and best in the world. Most of the books were made of the pith of the papyrus or paper plant. They were written in Greek and Latin.

Ptolemy appreciated the intelligence and learning of the Jews. He treated them with so much kindness and gave them so many liberties that great numbers of them settled in Egypt.

Two things that Ptolemy Philadelphus did are especially worth remembering. One was to commission a Greek translation of the Hebrew books of the Old Testament by seventy Jewish scholars. This translation was called the Septuagint (from the Greek word for seventy). The other notable acomplishment of Ptolemy was to open again a great canal which had been dug many centuries before from the Nile to the Red Sea. This canal was later filled up by the drifting sands of the desert and disappeared. It was not until the twentieth century that a new canal, the Suez Canal, was built to link these two bodies of water.

Ptolemy's canal connected the Atlantic with the Indian Ocean. Ships could sail from the Atlantic across the Mediterranean, then through the canal and the Red Sea, and on to India.

At that time Egypt raised more wheat than any other country in the world, so she had a great commerce. In exchange for her wheat she bought the products of Europe and Asia, and Alexandria became the richest city of the world.

But more than that the Ptolemies, especially Philadelphus, invited learned men to their court and gave them support so they might carry on their own studies and teach others.

At one time there were 14,000 students receiving instruction in the city. Thus Alexandria became the home of learning. It was there that pupils were first taught that the earth is round. One of the great astronomers who lived there found out very nearly the length of the earth's circumference and diameter. The people of Alexandria knew more about these things two hundred years before Christ than the people of Europe did a thousand years after. The science of today is only a continuation of what was begun by the wonderful Greeks whom the Ptolemies gathered about them in Alexandria.

One of the Ptolemy line was the celebrated Cleopatra, an able ruler and the most fascinating woman of her time. You can read something of her history in Famous Men of Rome, a companion volume to this book.

Chapter XXIX

PYRRHUS

Part I

A prince named Pyr´rhus lived in the state of E-pi´rus not far from the home of the great Achilles. At twelve years of age he became king, but the government was carried on for him by guardians.

About that time he read the story of Alexander the Great, and determined to be, like him, a great conqueror. While he was dreaming of victories in foreign lands, war came to him in his own country, and he was driven from Epirus. Ptolemy of Egypt helped him to defeat his enemies and regain his throne. Then he resolved anew to conquer as Alexander had conquered. He began with Alexander's own Macedonia. After a war that lasted several years, he got possession of one half the country. One of Alexander's generals took the other half. However, the people in Pyrrhus' half preferred to have the old general rule them. In seven months Pyrrhus had to give up his Macedonian kingdom.

He reigned quietly in Epirus for a few years. Then a chance came to try to conquer the Romans who lived just across the Adriatic Sea. Pyrrhus was delighted. Ruling Epirus was a dull business. In the south of Italy a great many Greeks had settled. Greek was the language of the people there, and the region was even called "Great Greece."

Rome wished to rule all Italy, but those Greeks were not willing to be under Roman rule. They sent word to Pyrrhus that they were in trouble and would like him to help them.

Preparations for war were made at once. As soon as possible, Pyrrhus landed on the shores of Italy with an army of about 30,000 men and twenty elephants.

A great battle was fought, and Pyrrhus won the victory. The loss of life, though, was dreadful. As he walked among the dead after the battle, he said, "Another such victory, and I shall have to go home alone." Half of his men were slain.

However, the Greeks of South Italy furnished him with fresh soldiers, and he gained a second victory.

The war came to an end in a very curious way. One of the servants of Pyrrhus deserted to the Romans and offered to poison his master for the consuls. The consuls sent the deserter back to Pyrrhus under guard with a message that they scorned to gain a victory through treason.

Pyrrhus, to show his gratitude, then sent all the prisoners he held back to Rome. This made the enemies friends, and a truce was concluded. One of the terms of the truce was that Pyrrhus should leave Italy.

A large number of Greeks lived in Sicily. They had built Syracuse and other large cities and towns. At that time the African city of Carthage was a powerful city. The Carthaginians were trying to conquer the Sicilian Greeks. Pyrrhus crossed to Sicily to help his countrymen.

But his Italian friends got into trouble with the Romans again. They begged him once more to help them. Accordingly, he left Sicily and went back to Italy. Now, however, his good fortune forsook him. He was totally defeated by the Romans under Ca´ri-us Den-ta´tus and forced to leave Italy.

He now returned to Epirus. As Pyrrhus was no lover of peace, he soon went to war a second time with Macedonia. Once more, he conquered the land of Alexander, but again the king of Macedonia regained the kingdom.

Not content to rule Epirus, Pyrrhus next went into the Peloponnesus and fought against the Spartans. They drove him from their territory.

Finally, he went to Argos and took part in a civil war which was going on in that state.

A fight took place in one of the streets of Argos. During it, a woman threw a tile from the roof of her house. It struck Pyrrhus on the head and stunned him. Some of the soldiers of the party he was fighting ran up and killed him (272 B.C.).

Part II

Sicily, about whose struggle with the Carthaginians you have just read, was the home of a famous mathematician named Ar-chi-me´des. He was born at Syracuse in 287 B.C., and was only a boy when Pyrrhus was in Sicily. Many years later, Syracuse was besieged by another enemy, the Romans. Archimedes, then an old man, proved of great help to his countrymen. He invented engines for throwing stones at the enemy. By using these engines the Sicilians kept the Romans at bay for a long time.

It is said the Archimedes set fire to Roman ships with powerful burning glasses. At last however, Syracuse fell, and Archimedes was put to death by a Roman soldier even though the Roman commander had ordered otherwise.

Chapter XXX

CLEOMENES III

Part I

About a hundred years after the death of Alexander the Great lived a young prince named Cle-om´e-nes. His father was one of the kings of Sparta and bore the name of one of the greatest Greek heroes, Leonidas, the famous defender of Thermopylae. One day, when the prince was about eighteen years old, he started from home to go hunting. He had not gone far from the city gate when one of his father's slaves overtook him and handed him a writing tablet. On its waxed surface Cleomenes read the words, "Leonidas, the king, to Cleomenes: Come back to the palace the moment you have read this note." Cleomenes turned and went back toward the city.

Late in the afternoon he reached the palace. The gateway was hung with a garland of flowers. Entering, he found the women busily arranging roses and lilies in every room.

As soon as he saw his father, he asked, "Is anyone going to be married?"

"You are," replied his father. "This evening I wish you to marry Agiatis, the widow of King A´gis. I am having the palace decorated for the wedding. She is beautiful and good and the heiress of one of the richest men in Sparta."

"But," said Cleomenes, "how can she ever be willing to marry your son?"

"I am the king," replied Leonidas, "and she is bound to obey me."

"Since you wish it, I will marry her," said Cleomenes, "but I do not believe that she will ever love me."

Cleomenes had good reason for saying this, for Leonidas had caused his fellow king, Agis, the husband of Agiatis, to be murdered.

Agis had been one of the best and greatest of Sparta's kings. He had been distressed at the state of his country when he came to the throne. The old customs of Lycurgus had been set aside. Since the close of the Peloponnesian War, when Sparta had proved more than a match for Athens, a great change had come over the kingdom. Her men were no longer warriors. The hope of Agis was that he might persuade the people to live according to the old laws which no one now obeyed.

But Leonidas, his fellow king, did not wish to return to the old ways of living, and the five ephors, or magistrates of Sparta, were friends of his. They determined to put Agis to death. The ephors seized him upon the street and carried him to prison, and — for no other reason than that he had tried to carry out the laws of Lycurgus and restore the glory of Sparta —he was put to death.

This had been done at the order of Leonidas. Cleomenes therefore had reason to think that Agiatis would never marry him. However, the marriage took place as Leonidas wished, and although Agiatis hated Leonidas for murdering her husband, she soon learned to love Cleomenes. Cleomenes was manly and true, and he devoted his life to making her happy.

She talked to him of Agis and what he had hoped to do for Sparta. As Cleomenes listened, he made up his mind to do just what Agis had wished to do. He saw that luxurious ways of living had weakened Sparta and destroyed her influence. And he saw also that his father's friends were not the few good and brave men still left in Sparta, but rich men who cared for nothing but money and pleasure.

Part II

Leonidas died a few years after the murder of Agis, and then Cleomenes became king.

At this time a great general named A-ra´tus was at the head of a league of Greek cities called the Achaean League. It seemed likely that it would soon control all the Peloponnesus. Cleomenes therefore persuaded the Spartans to go to war against the Achaeans.

In several battles he defeated Aratus and owned for himself great fame as a soldier. This made the Spartans very fond of him. He thought that the time had arrived when he might persuade them to obey once again the old laws and customs.

But the ephors were opposed to the changes which he wished to make. Cleomenes boldly put them to death.

The next day he banished eighty citizens who were opposed to his plans. He then explained to the people why he had done this, and why he had put the ephors to death.

"If, without bloodshed, " he said, "I could have driven from Sparta luxury and extravagance, debts and usury — the riches of the few and the poverty of the many — I would have thought myself the happiest of kings."

He declared that the laws of Lycurgus must be enforced and the land be again divided among the citizens.

The people were delighted when they heard all this. They were even more pleased when Cleomenes and his father-in-law were the first to give up their lands for division. The rest of the citizens did the same, and so, six hundred years after Lycurgus, there was a new division of property. Once more every Spartan had land enough to raise wheat and oil and wine for his family for a year.

Again the citizens dined at public tables on simple Spartan fare, and the youths were trained and drilled as Lycurgus had ordered. The Pyrrhic Dance, with trained soldiers in quick movements, was revived. Again the army was well disciplined, and the soldiers of Sparta became, as long ago, the best among the Greeks. The king himself set his people an example of simple living.

Some of the Greeks had laughed when Cleomenes said he would walk in the steps of Lycurgus and Solon. But when they saw Sparta victorious on the battlefield, and the city prosperous and happy once more, they could not help admiring the man who had brought the change about.

But in time a dreadful disaster befell Cleomenes and Sparta. The Achaean League invited the Macedonian king, Antigonus, to bring an army to help them against Cleomenes. In a single battle the Spartans lost almost everything they had gained.

The other king, Cleomenes' own brother, was killed, and out of six thousand men whom he had commanded, only two hundred men survived.

Cleomenes made his way to Sparta and advised the citizens to submit to the Macedonians, which they did, and the independence of Sparta was gone forever.

Cleomenes had hopes of getting help from Ptolemy, king of Egypt. So he sailed to that country, and he was promised assistance. But, unfortunately, Ptolemy died. The next king made Cleomenes a prisoner, because an enemy of the great Spartan had said that he was plotting against the Egyptian king. Cleomenes saw no way of escape and so put an end to his life.

Chapter **XXXI**

THE FALL OF GREECE

The states of Greece tried again and again to throw off the Macedonian yoke. Unfortunately, however, they often quarreled with one another and were not united against Macedonia. For this reason, the kings of that state kept their place as masters of Greece for another hundred years.

Then the Romans invaded the country, and the Macedonians were defeated in a battle fought near a town called Pyd´na. Their king Perseus was taken prisoner, and the Macedonian kingdom came to an end. Macedonia was made a part of the Roman Empire, and men were sent from Rome to rule it.

Epirus was captured next. A hundred and fifty thousand of its inhabitants were sold into slavery. The state was made into a Roman province.

After the fall of Macedonia, the other Greek states continued to fight with one another. About twenty years later (146 B.C.), a Roman army was sent against them. A battle was fought near Corinth. There the Greeks were completely defeated.

At that time Corinth was one of the richest cities in the world. After the battle, the Roman general let his soldiers enter the houses and take whatever they pleased. Pictures, marble statues, and jewelry were taken and shipped to Rome. It is said that two of the rough Roman soldiers played a game of dice on one of the finest pictures — so little did they value works of art.

Two thousand of the men of Corinth were put to death by the Romans, and the women and children were made slaves. After the buildings of the city had been plundered, they were set on fire.

Thus Athens, Thebes, Sparta and the other Greek states became, like Macedonia, parts of the Empire of Rome.

During the Middle Ages Greece passed from the rule of Rome under the rule of Turkey. In 1848 Greece revolted and became an independent nation once more.

If you ever go to Greece, as thousands of people do, to visit the places where her great men lived, you will see little but ruins. The columns of the temples are broken. The stones of their walls lie scattered on the ground.

And yet Greece, even amid ruin and decay, is still teaching the world. Many of the words that stand for branches of learning in our language today are Greek words. Such words include **arithmetic** and **mathematics**. They show plainly that the first teachers of mathematics in Europe were Greeks. **Gymnasium** and **athletics** are also Greek words. They show that the Greeks set us the example of running races, wrestling, jumping, throwing quoits and doing other such things to keep our bodies strong. **Poet**, too, and **poem** come from the Greek language, and so we are reminded that the Greeks also valued poetry. **Grammar, rhetoric, geography, logic, astronomy, surgery** and hundreds of other words used by us daily show us how much we have inherited from the Greeks.

Although the glory of Greece has waned, much of her learning and history were avidly studied during the Middle Ages and especially the Renaissance. Many of the Greek´s political ideas were very influential models for the men who wrote the United States' Declaration of Independence and Constitution. Much of what the Greeks achieved is still a part of our culture today.

What to do about Mythology...

T he "mythology" issue is one we have thought a lot about. Christian parents have legitimate concerns about teaching mythology. We don't want to teach falsehoods to our children (or lead them to confuse falsehoods with the truth); and we don't want to encourage any fascination with or inappropriate attention to the occult.

Having said that, we think that the study of mythology (Greek, Roman, Egyptian, and Norse) is still appropriate and profitable for our children when set in the proper Christian context for three reasons: It inoculates them against false religion; it gives them a deeper understanding of Greek and Roman culture (and Egyptian and European); and it builds a foundation for them to understand the great literature of western civilization.

The key phrase in the paragraph above is "the proper Christian context." Whenever we approach the topic of mythology, we introduce it by reviewing with our children what God has to say about the history of religion. Modern man spins a tale about primitive man beginning by worshipping anything and everything; trees, rocks, thunder, streams, grasshoppers, etc. Then the wisdom (foolishness) of the moderns speculates that man "progressed" to worshipping only a few specific deities. Then, as he began to walk completely upright, he moved from many gods to monotheism, the worship of only one god. The last step in this sequence you won't find spelled out explicitly, but it is the logical completion of the "evolution of religion" and that is the step from monotheism to atheism, the worship of no god. But this account of the history of religion is fales. The progression, from many to few to one to none, is not found in scripture anywhere. Beware of authors who present this as the way man's religions developed.

The Bible says that men fall into false religion and the worship of idols when they reject the truth about God, refuse to honor him, exchange the truth for a lie and suppress the truth in unrighteousness. There's nothing here about "progressing" towards God by way of mythology.

Our recommendation is not to teach mythology until you have taught Genesis. And when you study mythology, begin by reviewing with your children what God says about man's religion in the book of Romans. Once set in proper context, there are valuable lessons to be learned by reading the Greek myths. Without setting it in context, you risk confusion and error.

There is Biblical precedent for the study of other religions. Moses clearly knew Egyptian religious stories, Daniel mastered all of the writings of the Chaldees, and Paul clearly knew about Greek and Roman religion. This can be seen in the way each of them deals with the false religions of their culture. To understand the conflict between Moses and Pharaoh, it is tremendously helpful if you understand the relationship between the plagues and the Egyptian pantheon. It turns out that each of the plagues is God's challenge to a specific Egyptian deity. If you don't know who the Egyptian deities are, you can't fully understand what God is saying and doing.

This does not mean that we need to dwell on detailed descriptions of immoral practices associated with the false religions. We use common sense... and rely for the most part on texts published before 1965! But a study of the themes and major characters of Egyptian, Greek, Roman, and Norse mythologies will have much to teach us and our children.

The best protection we can give our children from false religion is an early inoculation/exposure to it under controlled circumstances. Set in context as described above, we have an opportunity to discuss with our children the contrast between true and false religion. We can highlight the foolishness of the false gods. They will always remember the comparisons and will be much less likely to be taken in by "new age" repackaging when they are older.

To understand the Greeks, Romans, Egyptians, or Europeans, you need to understand what they believed about their gods. By including a study of the myths when you read biographies or study these cultures you can ask key questions about how the false religion affected the culture. You can ask, "If the Greeks believed the gods behaved this way, how do you think they would behave themselves?"

The Romans adopted the Greek gods, and then went further and began to deify the emperors. Christians who refused to sacrifice to the emperor found their lives in danger. Note well, it was not illegal to worship Jesus; it was illegal to worship Jesus only! The worship of the emperor fit Roman "statism" very neatly and meshed with the respect all Romans were taught towards "the fathers" (Latin, "patria", whence we get our English word, "patriotism"). We cannot fully appreciate the issues facing early Christians unless we are familiar with Roman religion.

The myths are an integral part of our literary heritage. The great works of literature in the western tradition all use symbols and images drawn from the myths of the Greeks, Romans, and Scandinavians. We cannot appreciate the nuances or the ideas themselves unless we recognize the references. Knowing them does not mean we must accept them as true. But we should know them in order to intelligently converse with and present the Gospel to our culture. An acquaintance with the myths of the Greeks, Romans, and Norsemen has seldom proven a snare to adult Christians or their children. Quite the opposite seems to be true. For scholars like C.S.Lewis and J.R.R.Tolkien the myths and legends (what Lewis called "northernness") aroused in them an appreciation for beauty and drama and a longing for "Joy". A longing that Lewis said was instrumental in his final conversion to Christianity.

Our conclusion then? Do not teach mythology as a separate subject or in a way that encourages or entices. But do teach mythology as a key part of the history and culture of the Egyptians, Greeks, Romans, and Europeans. And do teach it in the context of what God himself teaches about man and his turning aside to false religions. In this way you will make your children better able to serve God, to communicate to the pagan culture around us, and to stand as Godly men and women in their own generation.

— Rob & Cyndy Shearer

A Few Words About Greenleaf Press

Greenleaf Press was founded by Rob & Cyndy Shearer in 1989. It was born of their frustration in searching for a history program for their children that was at the same time challenging, interesting, and historically accurate. What they were looking for was a curriculum that would begin at the beginning and present history in a logical, readable, chronological way. None of the available, in-print programs satisfied them. They discovered that the best history books for children they could find were, sadly, out of print. The best of the out-of-print classics were really terrific. They told interesting stories about real people. And the Shearer's discovered that their children loved history when it was presented in the form of an interesting story about a real person.

And so, they founded Greenleaf Press — to bring back to life some of the wonderful biographies which had been used to teach history so successfully in the past. The reprinting of Famous Men of Greece and Famous Men of Rome were Greenleaf's first publications. Those two books have now been joined by the reprint of Famous Men of the Middle Ages, Famous Men of the Renaissance and Reformation (written by Rob Shearer), The Greenleaf Guide to Old Testament History (written by Rob and Cyndy Shearer), and The Greenleaf Guide to Ancient Egypt (written by Cyndy Shearer).

Shortly after reprinting Famous Men of Rome, faced with questions from many people who liked the Famous Men books, but wanted help in HOW to use them, they decided to publish Study Guides showing how to integrate biographies, activities, and reference material. There are Greenleaf Guides available for Rome, Greece, and the Middle Ages, all written by Rob & Cyndy Shearer.

From that day to this, Greenleaf Press has remained committed to "twaddle-free", living books. We believe that history is both important and exciting and that our kids can share that excitement. We believe that if our children are to understand the roots of our modern-day, mixed-up world, they must study history. We're also thoroughly convinced that studying history with our children provides us with a wonderful opportunity to reflect with them on moral choices and Godly character.

Teaching History with Greenleaf Press Curriculum

Seven Year Plan

1st Grade — *Old Testament (Historical Books: Genesis – Kings)*
2nd Grade — *Egypt (& Old Testament Review)*
3rd Grade — *Greece and Rome*
4th Grade — *The Middle Ages and The Renaissance*
5th Grade — *The Reformation and The Seventeenth Century (to 1715)*
6th Grade — *1715 to 1850*
7th Grade — *1850 to The Present*

Six Year Plan

2nd Grade — *Old Testament and Egypt*
3rd Grade — *Greece and Rome*
4th Grade — *The Middle Ages and The Renaissance*
5th Grade — *The Reformation to 1715*
6th Grade — *1715 to 1850*
7th Grade — *1850 to The Present*

Five Year Plan

3rd Grade — *Old Testament, Egypt, Greece & Rome*
4th Grade — *The Middle Ages and The Renaissance*
5th Grade — *The Reformation and The Seventeenth Century (to 1715)*
6th Grade — *1715 to 1850*
7th Grade — *1850 to The Present*

Four Year Plan

4th Grade — *Old Testament, Egypt, Greece & Rome*
5th Grade — *The Middle Ages, The Renaissance, and The Reformation*
6th Grade — *1600 to 1850*
7th Grade — *1850 to The Present*

Internet: www.greenleafpress.com
3761 Highway 109 N., Unit D
Lebanon, TN 37087
615-449-1617

Teaching History with Living Books
An overview of
GREENLEAF PRESS
Study Guides and History Packages

The Greenleaf Guide to Old Testament History

We are strongly persuaded that the history of Israel ought to be the first history studied by every child. This Guide outlines a daily reading program that works through all of the historical books of the Old Testament. The focus is on history — not theology. What is remarkable is that the historical books of the Bible always focus on a central character. The pattern of history in the Old Testament is built around a series of biographies and character studies. The Old Testament really could be subtitled "Famous Men of Israel." Thus, the Study Guide discussion questions focus on "What actions of this person are worthy of imitation?" "What actions should we avoid?" "What is God's judgment on this life?"

The 196 readings are intended to be used, one each day throughout the school year. Yes, we know that's a few more readings than most people have school days. Be creative. You could do more than one reading on some days, or you could continue the study into the summer or the next school year. The readings are designed to give the student (and parent/teacher) an overview of the history of Israel and an introduction to the key figures whose lives God uses to teach us about Himself and His character. These stories are intended for children in the elementary grades, and should be accessible, even to children in kindergarten or first grade (though they make a rich study for older children, even teens and adults)! If this seems surprising, the reader is reminded that God's plan for families is for fathers to teach these stories to their children. When God decrees in Deuteronomy 6:6-7 that "you shall teach them diligently to your sons and shall talk of them when you sit in your house and when you walk by the way and when you lie down and when you rise up," He is not referring to math facts and grammar rules. God's textbook for children are the stories from the Old Testament. He is specifically referring to the story of the Exodus from Egypt, but by implication He means the entire Old Testament. The Old Testament is God's textbook for children. This is the only textbook, quite probably, Jesus used during his education in the house of his parents. *Duration: One full academic year*

The Greenleaf Guide to Ancient Egypt

Ever wonder how Biblical history and Ancient Egypt fit together? Why was God so angry with Pharaoh anyway? This makes a perfect second history unit for students. Or, as an alternative, you could pause in your study of Old Testament history and study Egypt after you have finished the story of Joseph at the end of the book of Genesis. This unit has ten lessons, including one devoted to the rediscovery of Egypt and the development of the science of archaeology in the 19th century. There is also a lesson on the Exodus in the context of Egyptian culture. The main text for the study is the Landmark book, The Pharaohs of Ancient Egypt, which includes biographies of the following Pharaohs:

Cheops (builder of the Great Pyramid)
Hatshepsut (His Majesty, Herself!)
Thutmose III (the Napoleon of the
  Ancient World)

Aknaton (the monotheistic Pharaoh)
Tutankamon (the boy-Pharaoh)
Rameses II (Smiter of the Asiatics)
Duration: approximately 15 weeks

Famous Men of Greece

If you were to have asked a citizen of ancient Greece to tell you something about the history of his nation, he would have wanted to begin at what he would have considered to be the beginning. He would have begun by telling you about his gods and the myths and legends told about them. Even though the events described in the myths did not actually happen in the way the story says, the Greek myths will tell you much about what was important to the people who told them.

Greek culture forms the backdrop to all the events of the New Testament. Paul was educated not just in the teachings of the Rabbis, but also in the writings of the Greeks. He was able to quote from literature in his speech to the men of Athens. Many of the details in his letters become richer and more significant when understood in the context of Greek culture.

Famous Men of Greece covers the following chapters:

Introduction: the Gods of Greece	Lycurgus	Socrates
Deucalion and the Flood	Draco and Solon	Xenophon
Cadmus and the Dragon's Teeth	Pisistratus the Tyrant	Epaminondas and Pelopidas
Perseus	Miltiades the Hero of Marathon	Philip of Macedonia
Hercules and His Labors	Leonidas at Thermopylae	Alexander the Great
Jason and the Golden Fleece	Themistocles	Demosthenes
Theseus	Aristides the Just	Aristotle, Zeno, Diogenes, Apelles
Agamemnon, King of Men	Cimon	Ptolemy
Achilles, Bravest of Greeks	Pericles	Pyrrhus
The Adventures of Odysseus	Alcibiades	Cleomenes III
	Lysander	*Duration: approximately 15 weeks*

Famous Men of Rome

Rome was the political super-power of the ancient world. Rome history spans 500 years as a kingdom, 500 years as a Republic, and 500 years as an Empire (when Rome was ruled by military dictators who called themselves "Caesar"). It was the Pax Romana of the Empire that allowed the Gospel to spread rapidly to every corner of the earth. And it was the example of the Roman Republic which inspired the United States' Founding Fathers.

Famous Men of Rome covers the following individuals:

Romulus	Cincinnatus	Julius Caesar
Numa Pompilius	Camillus	Cicero
The Horatii and the Curiatii	Manlius	Augustus
The Tarquins	Manlius Torquatus	Nero
Junius Brutus	Appius Claudius Caecus	Titus
Horatius	Regulus	Trajan
Mucius the Left-Handed	Scipio Africanus	Marcus Aurelius
Coriolanus	Cato the Censor	Diocletian
The Fabii	The Gracchi	Constantine the Great
	Marius	End of the Western Empire
	Sulla	*Duration: approximately 15 weeks*
	Pompey the Great	

Famous Men of the Middle Ages

We come to a time when the power of Rome was broken and tribes of barbarians who lived north of the Danube and the Rhine took possession of the lands that had been part of the Roman Empire. These tribes were the Goths, Vandals, Huns, Franks and Anglo-Saxons. From the mixture of Roman provinces, Germanic tribes, and Christian bishops came the time known as The Middle Ages and the founding of the European nation-states.

Famous Men of the Middle Ages covers the following individuals:

The Gods of the Teutons
The Niebelungs
Alaric the Visigoth
Attila the Hun
Genseric the Vandal
Theodoric the Ostrogoth
Clovis
Justinian the Great
Two Monks: Benedict
  and Gregory
Mohammed
Charles Martel
Charlemagne
Harun-al-Rashid
Egbert the Saxon

Rollo the Viking
Alfred the Great
Henry the Fowler
Canute the Great
El Cid
Edward the Confessor
William the Conqueror
Gregory VII & Henry IV
Peter the Hermit
Frederick Barbarossa
Henry the Second and
  His Sons
Louis the Ninth
St. Francis and St. Dominic
Robert Bruce

Marco Polo
Edward the Black Prince
William Tell
Arnold Von Winkelried
Tamerlane
Henry V
Joan of Arc
Gutenberg
Warwick the Kingmaker
Duration: approximately 15 weeks (though many families supplement this study with literature readings and extend it to a full year).

Famous Men of the Renaissance and Reformation

The Middle Ages were not the "Dark Ages." Yet there had been substantial changes in Europe from 500 to 1300 AD. Rome and her Empire fell. The Germanic tribes moved into the old Roman provinces and established feudal kingdoms. Many of the Roman cities declined in population or were abandoned. Gradually, much of the literature and learning of the classical world was lost and forgotten. Around 1300, in the towns of northern Italy especially, a group of men began to devote themselves to the recovery and revival of the classical world.

As the men of the Renaissance completed their work of recovery, another group of men arose, devoted to reform of the abuses within the church and relying upon the texts and tools of scholarship developed by the Renaissance humanists. The Protestant Reformation marks the beginning of "modern" European history. During that time we see men and women of remarkable courage and ability devoted to restoring the church to Biblical patterns. There are triumphs and virtues to be imitated, and tragedies and vices to be avoided.

Famous Men of the Renaissance and Reformation covers the following individuals:

Renaissance
Petrarch
Giotto
Filippo Brunelleschi and
  Donatello
Lorenzo Valla
Cosimo D' Medici
Lorenzo D' Medici
Girolamo Savonarola
Sandro Botticelli
Leonardo Da Vinci
Cesare Borgia

Niccolo Machiavelli
Leo X (Giovanni De Medici)
Albrecht Durer
Michelangelo Buonarroti
Erasmus
Reformation
John Wyclif
Jan Hus
Martin Luther
Charles V
Ulrich Zwingli
Thomas Muntzer

Conrad Grebel & Michael
  Sattler
Melchior Hoffman, Jan
  Matthys & Menno Simons
Henry VIII
Thomas More
William Tyndale
Thomas Cromwell & Thomas
  Cranmer
John Calvin
John Knox
Duration: Approximately 15 weeks.

Graphical Timeline of Ancient History

by Robert G. Shearer
© 1996 Greenleaf Press

Key Dates
Israel
c.1900 B.C. – Joseph sold into slavery
c.1445 B.C. – The Exodus
c.1000 B.C. – Death of Saul, David becomes King
605-1344 B.C. – The Exile

Egypt
2500 B.C. – Khufu (Cheops) The Great Pyramid
1505-1484 B.C. – Queen Hatshepsut
1361-1344 B.C. – Amenhotep IV also known as Akhenaton
51-31 B.C. – Cleopatra

Greece
c.1200 B.C. – Siege of Troy
478-404 B.C. – Civil War between Athens & Sparta
356-323 B.C. – Alexander

Rome
753 B.C. – Founding of Rome
509 B.C. – Founding of the Roman Republic
100-44 B.C. – Julius Caesar
312-327 A.D. – Constantine
410 A.D. – Sack of Rome by the Visigoths
476 A.D. – Death of the last Roman Emperor

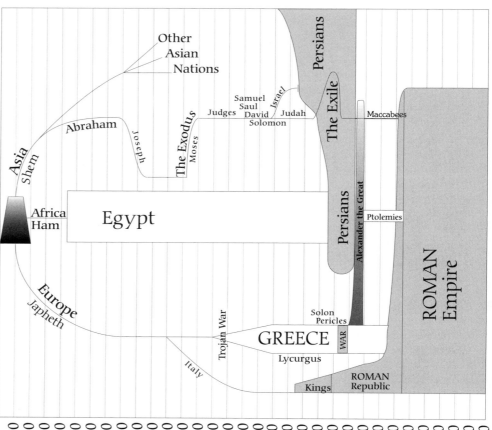

Graphical Timeline of Medieval History

Key Dates
England:
c.400 – Romans withdraw
793 – Sack of Lindisfarne by Vikings
871-899 – Alfred the Great
1066 – Norman Conquest
1339-1453 – Hundred Years War
1455-1485 – War of the Roses

France:
482-511 – Clovis
714-41 – Charles Martel
768-814 – Charlemagne
1180-1223 – Philip II Augustus
1412-1431 – Joan of Arc

Germany:
936-937 – Otto I, the Great
1152-90 – Frederick I Barbarossa
1210-50 – Frederick II, Stupor Mundi
1493-1519 – Maximilian
1516-1556 – Charles V

Italy:
440-461 – Pope Leo I
480-543 – St. Benedict
590-640 – Pope Gregory
1073-85 – Pope Gregory
1200-1240 – St. Francis
1309-1378 – Babylonian Captivity (of the Papacy)
1378-1417 – The Great Schism

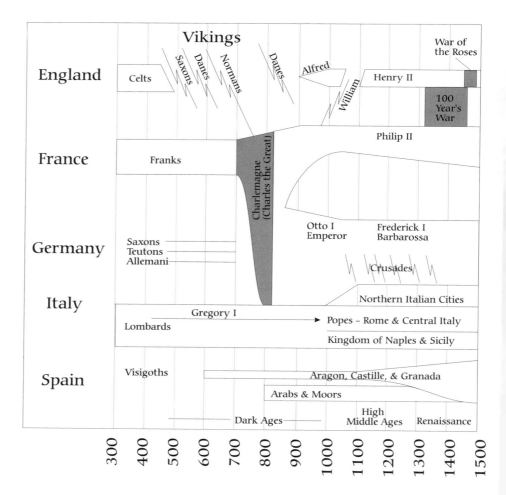